A Lamp Unto My Feet

A LAMP
UNTO
MY FEET

Guidance for Every Day

---

*"Thy word is a lamp unto my feet,
and a light unto my path."*

WALLACE FRIDY

ABINGDON-COKESBURY PRESS
New York • Nashville

A LAMP UNTO MY FEET

Copyright MCMLII by Pierce & Smith

Library of Congress Catalog Card Number: 52-11316

B

SET UP, PRINTED, AND BOUND BY THE
PARTHENON PRESS, AT NASHVILLE,
TENNESSEE, UNITED STATES OF AMERICA

TO MY WIFE

Martha Baskette Fridy

Whose Kindly Criticism Is Good for Me

Whose Faith Is an Inspiration to Me

FOREWORD

THESE messages were first delivered in amplified form as sermons. Later in their present abbreviated form they appeared in the Sunday edition of the *Spartanburg Herald-Journal* and thus reached a much wider audience.

They have emerged over a period of time and not overnight. They have come out of life's experiences. It is hoped that they may help illuminate the pathway of those who read them and become an inspiration for many a heavy-laden traveler.

This book was first suggested by a number of my readers who became a constant source of encouragement. I shall never forget their kindness and their words of appreciation. I am especially grateful to Phil Buchheit, publisher of the *Spartanburg Herald-Journal,* for the opportunity he afforded me in my weekly column and also for permission to use these little sermons in this book. To Mrs. John Iver Howell and Dr. Bernard Cannon for their patience in reading and correcting my manuscript, and to Mrs. T. S. Buie and Mrs. Frank Mann for their skill in typing and preparing it for publication, I am greatly indebted.

WALLACE FRIDY

CONTENTS

A LAMP UNTO MY FEET

"Thy word is a lamp unto my feet, and a light unto my path."   Ps. 119:105

SOME time ago I heard Martin Niemöller, the anti-Nazi Protestant clergyman, whose opposition to state totalitarianism landed him in a German concentration camp. He was put in prison for five years because he refused to acknowledge Adolf Hitler as a god. Niemöller said, "Jesus Christ is the only authority over the Christian Church." This was a threat to Hitler, so into a concentration camp went Niemöller and others like him who said, "God is my *Führer!*"

As he was talking, my mind went back to those fateful years when the secret police offered him freedom if he would only refrain from preaching, and, again and again, he refused. Once a prison mate told him how to bribe the guards and get lenient prison treatment, and Niemöller said, "I will not have a better fate than any other man in this camp."

In his address Niemöller said that of all his possessions taken from him he missed most the Bible. When an officer called the German pastor into his office and asked him if as a personal prisoner of Hitler he had any complaints, he replied, "Yes, let me have my Bible back!"

He told us that the experiences of the last two decades made him know that Christ is the living Lord—not just for today but for all time—and made him more convinced than ever before that no one can take his authority away.

11

It was during those days of misery and suffering that the Bible became living and real—a light in the darkness, hope in the storm. He found the promises Jesus gives in the Book, such as, "Lo, I am with you alway," to be real and true. He learned to trust his Word alone.

There are thousands of people today who bear witness to this same source of help and strength—the Bible. For unnumbered people it is a "lamp unto [their] feet, and a light unto [their] path."

I have in my possession a Bible that was given me by my grandmother. It is a book which I cherish very much, for I know that from this book she gained the strength and courage to face the trials and tribulations of her eighty-four years. Hardly a day went by when it was not opened, and out of it flowed into her life truth and comfort, and the very presence of God. Inscribed on the walls of her mind were its timeless truths. Imbedded in the innermost recesses of her heart were its assurances. Life for her was not complex. Death held no real fear. There were a mellowness and kindness about her life that came out of daily living with the Book and its priceless treasures.

Some time ago I was visiting in the hospital, and an elderly friend who was facing an operation said to me, "Please read to me from the Book." He knew that within it were words which could give him courage to face the unforeseen days which were ahead. He was confident that out of it could come a power which would help him to withstand the suffering and pains which would be his portion. When he went to the hospital, he not only took his toothbrush and pajamas, but there was also tucked into his bag his Bible, for he would be needing that too.

A columnist recently wrote:

This Book is perennially modern. It will never be outdated. At any price, it's priceless. For it brings solace to the sick, spiritual strength to the strong; it gives hope to the poor, humility to the proud. It has touched the heart of king and commoner. . . . If we keep our Bibles free from dust, we need worry less about keeping our weapons free from rust. And if we live by his teachings, we cannot fail to make Democracy live.

But let us never forget that this Book was not always an open Book, that our freedom to use it was bought with martyr's blood, that its life-giving strength comes only to those who open it and read.

It will serve no magic charm closed on our living-room table or tucked away in some dresser drawer. To take its place in our lives today, as it did in the lives of our forebears, it must be read and absorbed into our thinking and must become a guide in our living.

THE UNFAILING CURE

*"Let not your heart be troubled: ye believe in God, believe
also in me."*   John 14:1

WHEN Jesus said, "Let not your heart be troubled,"
he was not thinking of our automatic, tireless engine called
the heart; but he was thinking of the heart which we
often refer to as the seat of the spiritual or conscious life—
the soul or spirit.

When Jesus spoke these words to the disciples in that
upper room, they had reason enough to have troubled
hearts; for the upper room was shadowed with fear and
misunderstanding. They had the feeling that something
dreadful was in the making, that their world was falling
in, that all they had come to hold dear was going to be
taken from them.

For them there was something mysterious about the
upper room. There was a note of uncertainty in the air. Jesus
had told them that one would betray him and that another would deny him, and that the time had almost come.

The secrecy with which this meeting was planned, the
topics of conversation, the disturbing predictions of be-
trayal and denial—all served to fill them with a note of fear
and foreboding. They had reason enough for troubled
hearts.

Jesus knew that this kind of heart trouble brings with it
loneliness and fear. He felt their distress and said, "Let
not your heart be troubled: ye believe in God, believe also
in me."

14

How shall we face life when our hearts are troubled today?

In the first place we find that the constancies of earth and sky have quieted many troubled hearts. The Psalmist voices the feelings of us all when he says: "The heavens declare the glory of God; and the firmament sheweth his handywork. . . . The earth is the Lord's, and the fulness thereof; the world, and they that dwell therein."

The constancies of earth and sky calm our troubled hearts. Jeanbon St. Andre, a leader in the French Revolution, said to a peasant: "I will have all your steeples pulled down, that you may no longer have any object by which you may be reminded of your old superstitions."

"But," replied the peasant, "you cannot help leaving us the stars."

But when our hearts are troubled, as comforting as the stars and sky may be to us, we want more than that; for we know how cruel the forces of nature can be. The cyclone, the storm, the earthquake, wind, and fire—all can add to the troubles of our hearts.

So in the second place we have found the nearer constancies of dear and understanding friends to bring quiet to our hearts. How it helps to find a listening ear, to hear a familiar voice, someone to whom we may go and find understanding. All of us know what it means to have a friend in our presence in time of testing and trouble.

Addison said that "friendship doubles our joy and

divides our grief." Indeed it does! It calms our troubled hearts.

But we want more than earthly friends if our hearts are to be quieted.

This leads us to a final thought. Beyond the comfort which comes from the constancies of earth and sky, and from friends, Jesus points the way to faith in a support outside ourselves, a confidence that we are in the keeping of God's love and care. This is the unfailing cure.

When he said, "Let not your heart be troubled: ye believe in God, believe also in me," he was offering the only sure source of cure for troubled hearts.

This confidence that we are in the keeping of God's love and care is the sustaining assurance these words bring. They have been words of music bringing peace to troubled hearts since first they were spoken. "Let not your heart be troubled"—these are words beyond adequate comment, but their promise is never beyond acceptance, the promise of the unfailing cure.

FALLING IN LOVE WITH LIFE

"I am come that they might have life, and that they might have it more abundantly.   John 10:10

FOR many people life is not worth living. The cares of yesterday added to those of today and in anticipation of those of tomorrow are too much to bear. Life for a great many seems as it did for a character in one of John Galsworthy's plays—"a long headache in a noisy street."

> It is a tale
> Told by an idiot, full of sound and fury,
> Signifying nothing.

An author who entertains us with his stories, Somerset Maugham, who is thought of as one of the most lovable men of today, sums up his final creed about life with: "There is no reason for life and life has no meaning." There are people who deep down feel that life has no meaning.

Over against such despair we are looking for something which will give new hope and a new lease on life. Certainly we feel that unless there is more to life than we sometimes suspect, then indeed it is not worth living. Unless the way to which Jesus pointed is real, there is little hope for any of us. Time and again we come to an impasse which confronts us with the fact that we cannot carry on in our own strength. The strains of daily living, the misunderstandings in our home, burdens that grief places upon us, the temptations that easily beset us weigh heavily upon us and break us unless we turn to the "everlasting arms" which can hold us up.

There is a lovely story told by Robert Herrick in his book *The Master of the Inn*. A successful doctor, weighted down with the strains of a heavy practice in a large city, seeks refuge in a little village. There he buys an old house and turns it into a sanctuary for others who have been broken by the cares of modern living. These bruised from all walks of life come to him for help and health. Through a treatment of simplified living, physical toil, and spiritual care they are remade. The old doctor has suffered much, seen a lot, and developed spiritual resources which overflow into the lives of others. In recommending him one day a young surgeon says to a friend who needs help, "The doctor is a man who takes a person who doesn't want to live and makes him fall in love with life."

Our Lord is one who does exactly that. In him we find a power that can take a man who doesn't want to live and make him fall in love with life. In the tenth chapter of John, the tenth verse, he declares, "I am come that they might have life."

We see his power at work in those early disciples. After the crucifixion they scattered in despair. They knew not which way to turn, for the light of their life had gone out. Peter was brokenhearted over his denial and the others weighted down for having run away. But after that first Easter morning a new power came into their lives, for they knew their Lord had risen and was with them always. They became men of strength, joyous and overflowing with life. The blind George Matheson wrote:

Son of man, whenever I doubt of life, I think of thee. Nothing is so impossible as that thou shouldst be dead. I can imagine the hills to dissolve in vapor and the stars to melt in smoke, and the rivers to empty themselves in sheer exhaustion; but I feel no limit in thee.

Clement of Alexandria paying tribute to the risen Lord said, "He has turned all our sunsets into sunrise." And Bernard of Clairvaux declared, "He has come to water dry places; to illuminate the gloomy spots; and to inflame with warmth those which were cold. He has quickened my sleeping soul."

Today this same spirit is waiting to touch our lives and put new meaning into them. He is one who turns sorrow into abiding joy, fear into courage, routine and dullness into thrilling adventure. He can take a man without a purpose and give him a reason for living, without direction and give him a cause worth dying for. Yes, our Lord takes those who do not want to live and makes them fall in love with life.

LOVELY MUSIC FROM UNLIKELY INSTRUMENTS

"Gather up the fragments that remain, that nothing be lost."   John 6:12

SOMEWHERE I have read the story of a great concert artist, a violinist who owned a priceless Stradivarius. Thousands of people were moved to heights of ecstasy by his playing. He was acclaimed by kings and commoners as a musician of real worth.

But some thought that with such an instrument he should play well. So one night with a packed house in front of him the violinist took a cheap violin without the knowledge of his audience and played an entire program of classical music. The crowd stood in applause, for once again he had lifted them upward by his artistry. Then he came back on the stage, took the instrument and broke it across his knee. They knew then that even more than the instrument was the man who played it, that lovely music can come from unlikely instruments.

Is not this a parable about life? The common can become uncommon; the lowly can bring forth great music; the handicapped can rise to amazing heights of achievement. Yes, great music does not always come from the finest instruments. The fact is that the most stimulating successes in history have come from persons facing the handicap of lowly birth, physical impediments, or other limitations. They have taken their limitations as part of life's game and played splendidly in spite of them.

But most of us today are too easily discouraged when some obstacle comes in our way. We are too easy to give up. Most of us are shooting under our possibilities. We are too easily satisfied with life and how things are going. To be sure, the instruments upon which we play do make a difference. These we cannot ignore. The outer facts of life do make a difference. Yet in spite of our limitations we need not be defeated.

Here is a man who wanted to be a pianist but was told at the Warsaw Conservatory, where he went as a youth to study, "You have no future with the piano. It is useless for you to try." He was told that his hands weren't formed right for piano playing. Nevertheless Paderewski struggled on. He went to another eminent teacher who, too, tried to discourage him by saying, "You might have been a great pianist if you had started early enough. It is too late now." But he didn't let the discouragement of his teachers nor his age stop him. He practiced seventeen hours a day. He played at times when his hands tortured him. He withstood the hostility and ridicule of many an audience, but he continued to fight. Finally the world came to sit at his feet in gratitude for a man who found that lovely music can come from unlikely instruments.

Oftentimes it is hard for us to see that God can take ordinary clay and fashion it into something like unto a miracle. Dwight L. Moody discovered the secret and wrote his discovery in the margin of his Bible: "If God is your partner, make your plans large." It is so easy to dream of what we would do if we were someone else, living in another place, at another time. But what we must do is to work with what we have here and now, with God as our partner, and know that lovely music can come from unlikely instruments.

STARTING OVER AGAIN

"They that wait upon the Lord shall renew their strength; they shall mount up with wings as eagles; they shall run, and not be weary; and they shall walk, and not faint."   Isa. 40:31

WHEN I was in high school, there came into my possession a book written by an insurance salesman. His name was Vashni Young and his book entitled *Let's Start Over Again.*

The introductory story was of an old man and his wife whose farmhouse had burned to the ground. Nothing had been saved. A neighbor friend came over and asked, "You lost everything, didn't you?"

"Yes, everything," the old man replied.

Then the neighbor said, "You still have your health."

"Yes," replied the farmer, "we are both healthy."

"And you still have your children."

"Yes," said the farmer, "we are proud of our fine children."

"You still have your friends."

"Yes," said the farmer, "our friends are wonderful to us."

"And you still have God."

"Yes," said the farmer, "God has been mighty good to us. I guess we haven't lost anything that's really worth while, so we will just start over again." They did start over again, building a smaller house more suited to their needs, amid the ashes of their former abode.

This is a parable about life. Most of us at one time or another are forced to build on the waste places of past experiences, to start over again with nothing but the ashes of failure left upon which to build.

Several years ago I stood in the Reims Cathedral in France just prior to the outbreak of World War II. Workmen were taking down the lovely rose window which had just been restored from the wreckage left by World War I. They told me that the stained-glass window was to be stored underground for protection. A philanthropist here in this country gave money for the restoration of that cathedral, and skilled artists took the broken bits of glass and fashioned them into a lovely window. It was a salvage job. Out of the wreckage left by fire and shell a cathedral was restored.

Many times you and I in life are forced to pick up the bits of broken glass left from some bitter and unfortunate experience and start life over again. And oftentimes, as in a beautiful mosaic, the varied colors can add to the beauty of a salvaged life.

In a real sense this is the message of Christianity—that a storm-wrecked life can be salvaged. One of the great glories of our faith is that a man can start over again, that he need never feel defeated, that no matter how far down he has descended in the scale of living, there is still hope. Jesus spent a major portion of his ministry in trying to set men upon their feet again. His message was one of hope to the shipwrecked, one of courage to the fallen. He told men that they need not despair, for God offered a new chance and a new lease on life.

Today when we face defeat or even disgrace, let us

remember that life can be salvaged, that the great Artist of life can take the broken bits of experience and fashion them into a thing of beauty. As the rose window in Reims was restored from broken glass into a work of art, so Christ can use your failures, your sins, your sorrows, and out of them help you start life over again.

PHOTOGRAPH AS YOU GO

"Behold, I stand at the door, and knock: if any man hear my voice, and open the door, I will come in to him, and will sup with him, and he with me."   Rev. 3:20

WHEN I was at Yellowstone National Park, it seemed that every second person I saw was taking pictures. Motorists stopped along the highway to get snapshots of black bears, erupting geysers, boiling pools, breath-taking falls, and stately mountains.

Certainly there is no lovelier spot to capture the wonders of nature than Yellowstone. Its variety of scenery and natural beauty is unexcelled.

A friend of mine told me that once he saw a sign concerning photography which made a lasting impression upon his life. It read: "Photograph as you go for you may never pass this way again."

All of us have seen things which later we wished had been captured in picture: the smile of a child, the setting of the sun, the color of a flower garden. But too often we passed by, waiting for another shot which never was made.

This tells us something about life. It suggests to us not to put off living but to live now. So often we wait for the right time to do that which we have longed to do, and life ebbs away before it is done.

The psychologist William Moulton Marston asked three thousand persons: "What have you to live for?"

The answers he received revealed that 94 per cent were simply enduring the present, waiting for the future. They were waiting for "something" to happen: waiting for children to grow up, waiting for next year, waiting until they could afford a trip, waiting for someone to die. Most of them were waiting for tomorrow, forgetting that all one ever has is today, because yesterday is gone and tomorrow never comes.

A friend told me that often in his life he and his family had done things which they really couldn't afford and had to sacrifice to do them. But then he added rather wistfully, "I'm glad we did them for I lost my wife last year."

In our relationships with our friends and loved ones too often we delay in showing our love and affection until it is too late. With William Penn let us say, "I expect to pass through this life but once. If therefore there be any kindness I can show, or any good thing I can do to any fellow being, let me do it now, and not defer or neglect it, as I shall not pass this way again."

Then too we must learn to enjoy the process of our labors as well as the ends toward which we work. As practical and as necessary as it is to look forward to the completion of the task before us, we miss much of the joy of living if we fail to see meaning and deep satisfaction in the process of life.

Alice Freeman Palmer was one who found joy every day. She had three simple rules: commit something to memory every day—something good; look for something beautiful every day; and do something kind for somebody every day.

Finally this thought of photographing as you go suggests

to us something about our relationship with God. God is continually knocking at the doors of our hearts, continually seeking to get into our lives. "Behold, I stand at the door, and knock: if any man hear my voice, and open the door, I will come in to him, and will sup with him, and he with me."

It suggests to us to open the door and do it now. Invite him in, and your life will be full and radiant. When God prompts you, act at that moment for you may never have the chance again.

"Photograph as you go for you may never pass this way again."

MORE THAN CONQUERORS

"In all these things we are more than conquerors through him that loved us." Rom. 8:37

BACK in 1940 a Finnish pastor wrote to a friend in America these words: "My wife and I have lost our home. It went in the last air raid. Nothing could be rescued. My library, my documents, furniture—all lie in smoking ruins. But do not worry. We are still living, and that is the main thing. It is something great just to be a Christian in these times."

This man surely had found truth and meaning in the words of Paul when he said: "Who shall separate us from the love of Christ? shall tribulation, or distress, or persecution, or famine, or nakedness, or peril, or sword? . . . Nay, in all these things we are more than conquerors through him that loved us." These words do not represent victory after the battle of life as much as they represent hope and courage and faith in the battle. They portray for us the spirit in which the battle of life is to be fought.

This is what the Christian faith should do for a man. Henry Drummond was thinking of such when he said to students at Yale University: "We come not to save your souls, but to save your lives. . . . We want you to be Christians, not because you might die tonight, but because you are going to live tomorrow."

Being more than conquerors through Christ that loves us suggests that God's love cannot be affected, that it is unchanging and unalterable. Paul is saying that nothing can destroy this love as revealed in Christ. Regardless of what we do, God still loves us. When we please him with righteous living, he loves us. When we displease him in sinful living, he still loves us. His love is not dependent upon our deeds, our acts, our thoughts, our love.

To be sure, God, like an earthly parent, is pleased with goodness and kindness, but his love for us is unaltered by our living. Nothing we can do affects it.

Again, God's love cannot be bought. It cannot be purchased. We cannot buy his love any more than a child can buy the love of a parent. It is a gift. It is free. It is real.

Sometimes we are like the elder brother who, thinking he could buy favor with his father, said, "All these things have I done, and look." He imagined by doing good things he bought his father's love. Trying to buy a commercial relationship with God is a fear relationship and not one of love. Some of us say, "God, I'll do this if you do that." But you cannot strike up a bargain with him. His love is something to be received and not to be bought.

Although God's love cannot be affected, our response to that love does affect us. Whether we refuse or accept it, whether we respond by giving our love in return or by withholding it, this makes all the difference in the world.

If we deny or ignore this love, we suffer the consequences. We cannot escape the consequences of wrongdoing. When we refuse to accept and to give our love in return, we must accept the verdict of a New York taxi driver at the outbreak of the war who said, "We had it coming to us."

You remember how the young doctor in A. J. Cronin's *The Citadel* came to his time of reckoning. When politics defeated his health measures in a Welsh mining town, he sold his standards for money. After his wife's tragic death he found in her handbag snapshots of himself in those heroic days, and letters of gratitude from impoverished miners, and other mementos she had which reminded her of the man he might have been. He shouted to himself in a drunken stupor. "You thought you could get away with it. You thought you *were* getting away with it. But by God! you weren't."

Refusing to accept God's love by withholding ours always brings a dilemma. It brings judgment. His love is not variable, but the results of our response to it are. If we give genuine love back as a response to his love, life is wonderful and glorious, even in its tragedies. If we try to please him who loves us, our life will be victorious. If we accept this supreme gift as our own, depend upon it, respond to it, then we shall become more than conquerors through him that loved us.

So, in the words of Drummond, let us be Christians, not because we might die tonight, but because we are going to live tomorrow. And to live today and tomorrow we need that power which will enable us to become more than conquerors through him that loved us.

ATTENDING CHURCH

"And, as his custom was, he went into the synagogue on the sabbath day, and stood up for to read."   Luke 4:16

SEVERAL years ago one of our diplomats to a European nation was speaking in Chicago and picturing the terrible hour in which we live. A man in the audience asked if he saw any hope for civilization. To the surprise of all the diplomat answered, "The only hope is the Christian Church." How many of us honestly believe that the Church has the answer to the world's ills and evidence our belief by regularly attending church?

The first picture we have of Jesus after birth is one in the temple at the age of twelve, talking to the wise men and doctors. Again we find Jesus entering Nazareth, where he had been brought up; "and as his custom was," it is recorded in Luke, "he went into the synagogue on the sabbath day, and stood up for to read." That phrase "as his custom was" gives us a clue to his firmly fixed habit, but it is a habit that if persistently neglected will lead to moral decay and spiritual indifference. We make it of light importance, but it is of major seriousness, for going to church is more than a habit.

In the first place we should go to church because it provides spiritual rest and uplift. Who of us does not need, especially in days like these, our inner life rested, uplifted, charged, inspired? When Jesus said, "I have meat to eat that ye know not of," he was thinking of spiritual food, which literally brings nourishment to tired and fatigued bodies. It was his "over and above," his extra something, which saw him through. It was a reserve ready for tapping in hours of need.

There is the story told by Henry Sloane Coffin of a nurse, superintendent of a large hospital in New York City, who came to the end of a month's epidemic of influenza with a depleted staff of nurses and, having worked for nearly twenty-four hours, said to a subordinate, "I'm all in. I must consult a nerve specialist or"—and she doesn't know why she said it, for she had not been to church for years—"go to church." The next evening, against the advice of friends who wanted her to see a doctor, she entered the church, had her nerves quieted by soft music, listened to a sermon, took her mind off herself, centered it on God. Back at the hospital and after a few hours' rest she went bravely to her task, uplifted. Indeed, "our sufficiency is of God!"

Today we are torn and twisted by conflicting voices. Demands are crowding in upon us. Inwardly we are tornadoes. Outwardly we are all nerves. We desperately need one purpose, one voice, one will to follow, making all else fit together. Following his purpose for our lives is the only way to be whole. God made us for himself, and inwardly we are restless until we rest in him.

A second reason for going to church is that it is our duty as Christians to go. These lives of ours are not neutral in their effect upon people. They are either positive or negative, plus or minus. We either help or hinder, lift up or push down. Going to church is a silent witness to our faith in all that is good, our faith in God and his kingdom.

So our going to church throws our influence on the side of right and witnesses our faith in all that is good.

One other reason must be added. We should go to church because of our love for God and appreciation of his goodness to us. In other words it is our duty to God. From him come life and all that is worth while. Into our midst he has placed needed material out of which an abundant life may be had. He is indeed the creator, ruler, and sustainer of all that is.

God demands allegiance from you and me. "It doesn't," as someone has said, "take much of a man to be a Christian, but it does take all of him." God is a jealous God in this respect. "Thou shalt have no other gods before me." "Thou shalt love the Lord thy God with all thy heart, and with all thy soul, and with all thy mind." These are commandments we dare not disobey. His world is built so that if we neglect one of his laws, we suffer the consequences.

We should go to church for it is our duty to ourselves, to others, and to God. In the city of Chicago there is a little church on a dead-end street known as the Church at the End of the Road. Doesn't that suggest something to us? When you and I come to a dead end in life, when we face exhausting work, paralyzing trouble, insurmountable sorrow, when we come to the end of the road, we should go to church; for there God speaks to our needs and gives strength for our load.

TAKING LIFE FOR GRANTED

"Bless the Lord, O my soul, and forget not all his benefits."　　　　　　　　　　　　　　Ps. 103:2

YEARS ago King David fought his way to power. In his stronghold he was surrounded by the bravest of his captains, waiting to march on the Philistines, who had gathered for battle and were garrisoned at Bethlehem.

Just before the struggle David was musing upon home and friends. He was thinking of fig trees and vines that dotted the hills about Bethlehem. In thinking of his early days this thought slipped through his lips: "Oh that one would give me drink of the water of the well of Bethlehem, which is by the gate!"

Three of his faithful captains heard his low cry and broke through the enemy who were encamped about. They drew water from the well and took it to David.

David would not drink of it but poured it out to the Lord and said, "Be it far from me, O Lord, that I should do this: is not this the blood of the men that went in jeopardy of their lives?"

Here we have the drama of a gallant and unselfish service ending in an act of renunciation, which speaks to us all of deep and true gratitude. It is a story we might well keep in our minds.

It is so easy for us to take what is done for us for granted. It is sometimes our way to take what is handed to us and be unmindful of the price which others paid that we might

35

have it. It is a sin to be ungrateful. And without gratitude men will not walk long with God.

How easy it is for us when in good health, sheltered homes, and with well-fed bodies to take them for granted. All of us at times are guilty of this and often wait until misfortune strikes to be thankful for what is ours.

A lady said to me one day, "You know, a person doesn't know how to appreciate being able to see until his eyesight is threatened or impaired." Just try shutting your eyes and imagine you cannot see. Now open them and thank God that you can see.

Perhaps some of you are thinking that it is easy for the prosperous, the fortunate, who by heritage or achievement have been given the cushioned seats, to be really thankful. They, you may say, have something to be thankful for. True it is they do have something to be thankful for, but they are not always the most appreciative nor the personalities who have made life worth living.

From Jesus, poor, homeless, and crucified, on down to Helen Keller, the personalities to whom life has been most worth living have not been generally on the fortunate side of life; they have not sat on the easy seats of the world.

Think of all the gifts of life for which we should be thankful which are not for sale. The beauty of nature is a free gift. Sunrise and sunset, the sea, the mountains, the valleys—all are free to be gratefully taken and worthily used.

Our most beautiful human relationships are free gifts.

We did not pay for the motherhood that bore us nor for the care of fatherhood. All fine friendship and true love are free bestowals. One cannot buy them.

But the greatest of life's free gifts is that which God has given us, his Son, Jesus Christ. In him God revealed himself to mankind. But how often we take his life for granted and fail to realize his significance for our lives.

There is an old hymn that all of us are familiar with. Some of the words read like this: "Count your many blessings, name them one by one." What sane advice this is, for it does us good to stop and count our many blessings and then thank God for them.

THE GREATEST VIRTUE

"Well done, thou good and faithful servant: . . . enter thou into the joy of thy lord."   Matt. 25:21

WHEN one visits Yellowstone National Park, Old Faithful, the geyser, takes first place in point of interest. It is a magnificent sight, and it reaches at times, when erupting, a height of 171 feet. Its average duration is 4 minutes, and the interval between eruptions averages 64 minutes. Of course no two eruptions are the same, but each discharge brings forth from 10,000 to 12,000 gallons of water.

It is the most photographed geyser in the world and is especially beautiful at night when floodlights of many colors are focused upon it.

Old Faithful is not the largest geyser, nor does it reach the greatest height. Nevertheless it is by far the most popular geyser. Its popularity is due mainly to its regularity and dependability. You can count on Old Faithful. Nothing in life can take the place of faithfulness and dependability. It is one of the greatest virtues. Brilliance, genius, competence—all are subservient to the quality of faithfulness.

On any team a coach prizes the dependable player. Any pastor knows what magic is contained in these words, "Pastor, you can count on me." Any businessman knows what it means for a man's word to be his bond.

Success in any enterprise is dependent upon faithfulness and dependability.

Oftentimes I get inquiries concerning the character and fitness of a person seeking employment. Invariably this question is asked, "Can she be depended upon? Is he loyal? Will he be faithful to his duties?"

The way we handle the little jobs committed to our care determines our fitness to handle the big jobs ahead. It is this faithfulness in little things that determines our worthiness to handle, then, big things which come our way.

You remember the words of scripture which read: "Well done, thou good and faithful servant: thou hast been faithful over a few things, I will make thee ruler over many."

How the world today needs men and women who are faithful to the little tasks of life! There is a satisfaction which comes with faithfulness that comes in no other way. To know that you have done your best—such knowledge has no equal in life. No wonder the above scripture continues, "Enter thou into the joy of thy lord."

God is not expecting us to become great or famous. But he is expecting us to be faithful to him.

Life is really lent to us to be spent in God's service. We are to give the best that we have to the highest that we know. Then we too shall surely hear those words: "Well done, thou good and faithful servant: thou hast been faithful over a few things, I will make thee ruler over many things: enter thou into the joy of thy lord."

LIFT UP YOUR HEADS

"When these things begin to come to pass, then look up, and lift up your heads; for your redemption draweth nigh."
Luke 21:28

ALL over the world today there are men who are suffering and in trouble. There are millions who are sick. There are those living in broken homes. Many are without jobs. Others are disappointed in love. Every hour of the day thousands are losing friends and loved ones through death.

We find Jesus speaking to men of his day assuming that hardships would come upon them. He says, "When these things begin to come to pass, then look up, and lift up your heads; for your redemption draweth nigh."

There are many today who give up in defeat when trouble comes upon them. They can see no possible good in it. For them it shatters their faith. Yet for others this same trouble confirms their faith. For some the anxieties and sorrows of life destroy their hope in God, while for others the same anxieties and sorrows establish their hope in God.

Jesus says, "When these things begin to come to pass," do not give up in despair, feeling that all is lost, but rather "look up, and lift up your heads; for your redemption draweth nigh." He is saying that in your trouble and suffering God will either heal them or give you the power to overcome them.

If we look at our New Testament, we find that almost everything beautiful comes out of something ugly. Look at Paul's greatest poem, the thirteenth chapter of First Corinthians—"If I speak with the tongues of men and of angels, but have not love, I am become sounding brass, or a clanging cymbal." This great masterpiece was written while Paul was facing an uncertain future. Again, the most far-reaching event of all history, the Cross, came out of bitterness, hatred, and evil. God turned such an apparent defeat into a glorious victory.

So in the history of the Christian Church we find that its greatest moments of influence followed not periods of prosperity and ease, but rather when it was being persecuted like its Christ. It was when the Church's existence was threatened that its greatest influence was felt.

Over and over again in the life of today do we see defeat turn into victory in human lives. It was in London, when seriously hurt in an automobile accident, that a man took literally Jesus' words, "Lift up your heads." After the doctor had examined him, it was reported that sight could be partially saved in one eye but that a glass eye must replace the other. After a moment of resentfulness the man finally said, "Well, doctor, if you have to put in a glass eye, give me one with a twinkle in it." That's true greatness. Faith in Jesus makes men like that.

It is in moments like these—sickness, death, heartaches— that God draws nigh. When Jesus said, "For your redemption draweth nigh," he meant that in hours of trouble God comes very close to the human heart. It does not mean that he is not always close, but it means that we are so conditioned by pain and sorrow that we are ready to receive God and his love. In other words we lose confidence in our own strength and make ourselves ready to receive God's help.

It is when we are broken in spirit and humble of heart that God can come in and uphold us.

"When these things begin to come to pass," some men lose faith in God and give up in defeat; but others upheld by the Christian faith look up and lift their heads, for they know that their redemption draweth nigh.

WHERE GOD MEETS MAN

"He that hath seen me hath seen the Father." John 14:9

IN LLOYD C. DOUGLAS' book *The Robe* there is a conversation between two Roman soldiers who claim to have no religious faith. They do not believe in the many gods of Rome, but they confess that it would be good to have a god—one god—whom they could worship and to whom they could give themselves completely. Paulus then tells Marcelus what kind of god he would like. Here is what he says:

This god I am going to invent is good. He doesn't just pretend to be good. He really is good! He takes a few bright men into his confidence—not necessarily Romans or Greeks or Gauls; just so they're honest and intelligent—and entrusts them with some important tasks. He tells one man how to cure leprosy, and others how to restore sight to the blind and hearing to the deaf. He confides the secrets of light and fire; how to store up summer heat for use in winter; how to capture the light of day and save it to illumine the night; how to pour idle lakes onto arid land.[1]

If you did not believe in God and someone asked you what kind of God, worthy of your allegiance, you would invent, what would you say? What would be the nature of the god you would invent?

The idea of God is a stupendous concept, too big for the

[1] Used by permission of the publishers, Houghton Mifflin Co.

human mind to comprehend. Think of it: a God who has created this universe and now controls it. As we look out upon this marvelous world we know, and scientists tell us of distances and island universes millions of light-years away, we find new meaning in the Psalmist's exclamation, "The heavens declare the glory of God." When we think of these bodies of ours, their minuteness of detail, surely you and I must say with the Psalmist, "I will praise thee; for I am fearfully and wonderfully made: marvellous are thy works; and that my soul knoweth right well."

The mind of man is too limited to conceive of the greatness of God. So when we think of him, we have to use symbols. We lift up the highest in human experience to help us comprehend God. We call him a rock, a fortress, a bulwark, and a high tower. We call him Father, Companion, Friend. We call him Ancient of Days and Hound of Heaven. We say God is like this and God is like that. Hence we must conclude that our ideas of God are only partially true.

But we must not leave the matter here. Although God is so great that we conceive of him in symbolic terms, yet there is a way in which he touches us.

Each summer many of us go to the beach for a vacation. There we look upon the vastness of the sea. We do not know all of it. In fact many of us have never sailed out very far upon it. But no one can say that we do not know the sea, for we do. We know that which touches our beach.

We bathe in it, we sail in it, and we are lulled to sleep by its music at night.

God is like the sea. He is so great that we cannot know all about him, yet there is a way in which he touches us. It is this which is of most concern to us. To be sure, it is gratifying to think of a powerful God, a great God; but what you and I want to know most about is that part of God which washes our shores.

There are many ways in which God touches our lives—through beauty, truth, and goodness—but let us consider the supreme way in which he has revealed himself. In Luke 7:16 we have these words, "God hath visited his people." Here this doctor-writer Luke referred to Jesus, who came to live among men. He was saying what Paul said, "God was in Christ, reconciling the world unto himself." So in Jesus of Nazareth we find the face of God. We have but to look at him and we find the answer to our question, What is God like? for in Jesus Christ we find revealed the heart of the universe.

Looking at Jesus, men no longer need to say, "Shew us the Father, and it sufficeth us," for Jesus answered their request by saying, "Have I been so long time with you, and yet hast thou not known me? . . . he that hath seen me hath seen the Father."

In him God touches our little shores—the Christ who not only lived historically but also lives today. Here the divine and human meet, as God revealed himself in the life of Jesus Christ. Here God meets man—in Christ Jesus.

45

DANGEROUS SUPPOSITIONS

"But they, supposing him to have been in the company, went a day's journey; and they sought him among their kinsfolk and acquaintance. And when they found him not, they turned back again to Jerusalem, seeking him." Luke 2:44

THESE words relate to the well-known journey to Jerusalem when Jesus, boylike, became lost from his parents and was discovered where they left him—in the temple talking with the wise men and doctors.

You say what a strange thing for parents to do: supposing Jesus to be in their company and going a day's journey. But it is not so incredible or extraordinary that they did not miss him until after a day's journey. The Galilean pilgrims would travel together in a caravan, usually in large numbers. It was the custom for the elderly women and men to be mounted on camels and the younger men and children to walk. Frequently they would stop at some spring to feed the camels and refresh themselves with water, dates, melons, and cucumbers. It was a festive journey and a hilarious one for the children, who would play together and often go from one end of the caravan to the other. Sometimes they would be able to rest by mounting a camel whose load was less heavy than the rest. Thus the supposition that Jesus was in some other part of the caravan was a natural one.

But the point of this for us today is that we too can travel our day's journey, and longer, in life supposing Jesus to be in our company and suddenly discover that he is not.

In the first place, to suppose that the religious experience of another can suffice for one of our own is as dangerous as to suppose that the food another eats can give strength and sustenance to our bodies. No secondhand religion will do. We cannot inherit a religious experience.

To be sure, there are some things which we can inherit in religion. The church in which we worship is something which we have inherited, but it is the sort of thing which can be handed down from one generation to another. The hymnbooks we use are a part of a glorious heritage—a testimony to those who tried to express in words and music the heights and depths of their religious experience. Yes, schools, colleges, hospitals, orphanages, creeds, dogmas—all are products of the Christian faith and ours to use and pass on to future generations. But these are merely the clothes of Christianity, the fruits of past experiences, the crucibles containing the results of a vital faith of others and not a faith of our own.

In the second place, to suppose that being a Christian is just a matter of one decision is a dangerous supposition. Decision must follow decision; commitment must follow commitment. It is a "process of continual reaffirmation," as Edwin Lewis says, "and more is affirmed as more becomes realized."

To be sure, conversion settles the main question and the main direction. It points our feet in paths that we should follow. It is the great beginning. It is the major decision. But after it some people seem to stand still. Like Paul at

Damascus they fall to the ground, but unlike Paul they never arise.

It was Cromwell who wrote in the flyleaf of his Bible this truth, "He who is not getting better is getting worse." What a dangerous supposition it is to hold that the Christian faith is just a matter of one decision!

Finally, it is dangerous to suppose that we can hold him—the Christ—and act as if we have never found him. We cannot live like a pagan and still be a Christian. Our actions must measure up to our faith if we are to hold the faith. Having him makes a difference in how we live. Someone has said, "No one can well believe that our piety is sincere when our behavior is lax and irregular in its little details."

A cowboy was converted in one of Bud Robinson's meetings. Out of habit a few days later he dismounted in front of the town saloon and started to tie his horse to the hitching post. Just then Robinson came along and gave this advice, "If you are going to follow Jesus, you had better find a new hitching rail."

Yes, there must be in the quality of our living something fine and good and noble if we would hold on to a vital relationship with Christ. If we are dishonest in our living, we do not hold the Christ near to us.

Walter Russell Bowie tells of a minister who had been sent by his home church to the mission fields of Asia and who was on his homeward journey. The airplane in which he was flying came across the deserts to Damascus and then turned southward along the Mediterranean shore. Above all else he had wanted to see Jerusalem, but the pressure of time made it impossible. By his side sat a young aviator who knew every mile of this territory, and when he learned of the minister's desire to see the Holy City, he told him that at a certain point in the Judean hills, if conditions were right, they could get a far distance view of it. As they approached this point, they watched with concentration for the one moment of opportunity. The airplane swept onward; the hills flowed past them. They came to the gap, went past it, but there was no view of the city. "I am sorry," said the aviator. "We have lost our chance." And then in explanation he said what became a parable which the minister would never forget: "If we had been flying a little higher, we should have seen the Holy City."

PULLING OUT ALL THE STOPS

"For my people have committed two evils; they have forsaken the fountain of living waters, and hewed them out cisterns, broken cisterns, that can hold no water." Jer. 2:13

ONE Sunday evening I thought of what a wonderful day we had had in our church that day. I was pleased with our morning service and with the wonderful attendance at Sunday school. Then at the evening service my heart was made to rejoice.

When all these things coursed through my mind, this thought occurred to me: What would happen in our churches if we pulled out all the stops?

I understand that when all the stops are pulled out on a pipe organ, you then get full volume. Pulling out the stops gives full tone to the instrument.

So I thought of what would happen if all our churches set themselves to do this. I was not thinking primarily in terms of financial support, but particularly of being used as an instrument in the hands of God. When all the stops of life are pulled out and God is let in, what happens?

For one thing we discover that we need not more action but more power, power to lift. What a healing and lifting power would be let loose in the world through cleansed channels carrying God's love! If God can have his way with us, we can become a light set upon a hill.

It is easy for us to believe that just because we are doing things, we are doing what God wants us to do. Action can be a substitute for doing God's will. Just because yours is an active church does not mean that it is a dedicated church.

There must be purpose in our action and direction in our doing. Of course we all believe in an active Christianity, but once in a while we had better stop to see if we are going in the right direction and doing the right thing. We had better see if in our movement we have crowded out God.

I as a preacher must stop and see if I am being used effectively as an instrument in the hands of God when I preach. I must search my own soul to see if my motive is right and if I am getting out of God's way so that his truth and his message can reach the minds and hearts of men.

The church that seeks to do God's will and lets itself be used as an instrument of God will exert a power that will lift and mold and mend.

But too many of us have come to look on religion as a means of getting what we want rather than a means of helping us do what God wants. We think in terms of a "power religion" and the power to be used in getting what we want rather than in getting what God wants.

Joseph Fort Newton was standing near Niagara Falls one day with an eminent scientist, Washington Cooper, who said, looking at the falls, "The greatest unused power on earth."

"No," said Newton, "you are wrong. The greatest unused power on earth is the spirit of God."

"You are right," replied Cooper. "If only the church were

a school of spiritual technology, we could remake the world."

So in this noisy and turbulent age the church must discover that power is needed more than noise if it is to be a light in a darkened world.

Again, when we pull out all the stops and let God in, we discover that we cannot go further until we have gone deeper. This is true in our personal lives. It is true in our church life. Most of us cannot do more than we are now doing—that is under our own steam—but we must go deeper and tap wells with an unending source of supply.

We must learn to draw our strength not from artificial reservoirs but from living springs. This is what Jeremiah had in mind when he said, "For my people have committed two evils; they have forsaken me the fountain of living waters, and hewed them out cisterns, broken cisterns, that can hold no water."

This parable tells us a great deal about life. One reason that life for many people is not worth living is because they are drawing their living out of cisterns and their cisterns have run dry. When we go deeper, we open the valves of our souls to another world.

"Dick" Sheppard, the late dean of Canterbury Cathedral and rector of St. Martin-in-the-Fields, London, carried heavy burdens of responsibility and unhappiness, and yet he was always vibrantly alive. Ellis Roberts says of him: "The stream of unceasing refreshment which always flowed from him depended for its powers on deep hidden springs, on its renewal from the melted snows of lonely and distant heights of the spirit."

Too many of us are only half using the powers God has given us because we have not pulled out the stops and let him in. Dwight L. Moody said: "Let God have your life. He can do more with it than you can."

GIVING OTHERS A LIFT

"Be ye kind one to another, tenderhearted, forgiving one another, even as God for Christ's sake hath forgiven you."
Eph. 4:32

ONE day a woman in great distress came to me and said, "All I need is a job and a pat on the back." Maybe she needed more than that, but how a word of encouragement, a friendly greeting, a thoughtful deed, genuine praise —how far these go in giving us needed lifts in life.

One of the greatest needs in the world today is kindness and thoughtfulness. To be sure, in some quarters the world starves for food, for economic aid, for material welfare; but as great as this need is, that of love and kindness is greater. A kind word, a friendly handclasp, a token of encouragement—such lifts in unexpected places and from unexpected sources have often changed the course of many men's lives. It must have been this need about which Ian Maclaren was thinking when he wrote, "Let us be kind to one another for most people are fighting a hard battle."

When we think of our own lives and the encouragement which others have given us, we soon see that it has not always been a material gift which has renewed our confidence and hopes in life. Here, for example, is Thomas Edison, who made a miserable failure in school. His teacher said that he was addled and would never learn. This was all that was needed to destroy his self-confidence, and then his mother stood up for him. She convinced young Tom that he was not addled and that he had great possibilities.

It was this faith of his mother that made the difference in young Edison's life.

But it is not only mothers, fathers, and relatives who have given lifts to their kin; such privileges have been and are open to every one of us. Every day of our lives new opportunities present themselves through which by our kindness we may change the course of others' lives.

Restoring confidence in people is one of the greatest gifts we can give to another. One way to begin is by giving people lifts of encouragement, extending the hand of kindness. The great master Teacher was one who went about restoring confidence and self-respect in people who had lost all zest for living. Jesus saw beneath the rough exteriors of crude fishermen to their finer selves and helped to bring them out. He looked with tenderness and compassion, not condemnation, upon fallen women and caused them to want to be better. A Magdalene had her self-respect restored; a grafting tax collector, Zacchaeus, caught from him a glimpse of what he might become and restored what he had taken unjustly. Wherever Jesus went, his faith in men wavered not; and this faith in them engendered their faith in themselves.

It is so easy to see flaws in people, to pick out faults, to look for weakness in others. But what the world needs today is not more "faultfinders" but more "appreciators"—people who are not blinded to human failures but who look beyond to human virtues, people who lift up rather than push down.

GOING FROM BAD TO GOOD

"But Barnabas took him, and brought him to the apostles."
Acts 9:27

SOMEWHERE Theodore Parker Ferris has said that we often speak of a man going from bad to worse, but seldom do we speak of a man going from bad to good. Yet the heart of the gospel truth is that a man can go from bad to good, that human nature can change for the better.

Here is Paul whose record was bad. He had been relentless in persecuting Christians. He was on his way to Damascus to do that very thing, but something happened that changed him from a persecutor of Christ to one who preached that Jesus was the Son of God.

But his friends remembered his past and would not believe him. They said, "Is not this the man who has been putting to death the followers of Christ?" They thought he could not change overnight. He went to Jerusalem and thought that surely among Jesus' disciples he would find those who would believe in him. There he found the same hostility.

But fortunately we find in Paul's life a man who did not listen to common sense. In Jerusalem there was a man who believed in him. At the darkest moment in the story comes this line, "But Barnabas took him, and brought him to the apostles." What it must have meant to Paul at that moment to find one man who gave him the benefit of the doubt, who dared to gamble on his sincerity, who gave him a chance. Let us look more closely at this story.

For one thing we find that when Barnabas got behind Paul, he was expressing his faith that a man can change. It is very easy to be suspicious of men. It is sometimes hard to act as though we believe a man can change. "Human nature being what it is does not change," some say. But William Hocking says:

Human nature is the most plastic part of the living world, the most adaptable, the most educable. Of all animals, it is man in whom heredity counts for least, and conscious building forces for most. To anyone who asserts as a dogma, "Human nature never changes," it is fair to reply, "It is human nature to change itself."

Down through history there have been those people who have changed the direction of their lives. Before we give up all hope in man's changing, we had better remember men like Paul who changed the course of their lives.

In the second place Barnabas' believing in Paul made Paul believe in himself. He responded to such faith. It was just what he needed. Surprisingly enough in even the worst of us there is a response to such faith.

I have a friend who has spent his life giving others the benefit of the doubt. He has helped students through school. He has believed in students when others' faith failed. He has lifted men out of bad pasts into worthy futures. Trust in another has a certain transforming power about it. It helps to awaken a person to the good life.

And finally this is the story of Christianity—the story of

a God who gives us the benefit of the doubt. It is the story of one who takes a chance on men.

How many times we fail him, but he still believes in what we can become. Yes, it is the story of a God who is always willing to give us the benefit of the doubt, to forgive the sins and mistakes of the past, and who offers us a new chance to go from bad to good.

INVALUABLE IN SMALL PARTS

"He that is greatest among you shall be your servant."
                                                    Matt. 23:11

FOR days I have watched the construction of a twelve-story apartment building. I have marveled at its design and thought of its planners—the architects, the contractors, the draftsmen, the builders. Then I have watched the men who worked at simple jobs—those who dug ditches, poured the concrete, fitted the pipes, drove the nails. How essential they are, and how helpless the planners without the masons, the carpenters, the plumbers, the water boys—those workers at menial tasks.

Perhaps you have felt that the place you fill in life and the meager talents you possess are rather unessential in the world's work, for all of us have that experience at one time or another. But let us never forget that one of the greatest needs in the world today is for men and women, boys and girls, willing to play second fiddle that the concert might go on. It is the ordinary folks like you and me upon whom God is depending to make this world a better place in which to live.

To be sure, leaders are needed, prima donnas are necessary, presidents have to be elected, captains must run the team; but leaders without followers, prima donnas without supporting voices, presidents without workers, captains without teams—such would make an impossible world. Certainly we are impressed with the leaders of men—those five-talented people, the folks who do things and do them well. But we sometimes forget that behind them are unnumbered men and women in lowly walks of life who make the work of leaders possible. These are the people who are taken for granted and without whom nothing could be done.

Charles Brookfield was such a man. He had the unusual experience of being mistakenly reported dead. Of all the comments about his life this one he cherished above all: "Never a great actor, he was invaluable in small parts."

It takes a lot of grace and humility to take small parts, to play second fiddle, to be a blocking back, to stand in the shadows, to labor in the ranks. Surely it was of these Jesus was thinking when he said, "He that is greatest among you shall be your servant." He gives us a graphic picture of this when on the night that he was betrayed, he took a towel and a basin of water and washed the disciples' feet. The humble task, the menial job, the loving service—these are what count in the Master's eyes.

God is waiting for you to seek a place on his team. He may want to use you as a pinch hitter, a bat boy, a star pitcher, or even one who keeps the score. But if you are on his team and play your part well, whatever part you play, you will gain his cherished praises: "Well done, thou good and faithful servant: . . . enter thou into the joy of thy lord."

LIFE'S HEALING POWER

"In him we live, and move, and have our being." Acts 17:28

A WOMAN who had been confronted with many kinds of illness said to her doctor, "With all the germs and diseases that threaten man I do not see how we are ever well."

The wise doctor answered by saying, "Knowing the human body as I do, I wonder why we are ever sick."

This doctor was giving voice to what seems to be a universal truth in life, namely, that for all kinds of illnesses and bruises there seems to be a power at work that would heal. In the midst of broken hearts as well as broken bodies and distrupted nature there seems to be some healing power at work. Whether it is the healing of a limb sawed off a tree, the mending of a broken bone, or the renewing of a broken spirit, this restorative power or force is at work in our world.

When we reflect upon life, we can see that where there are forces that would destroy, there are also forces that would heal; where hearts are made sad by death, those same hearts —most of them—are healed by something in life. We can now discern that battle-scarred fields of yesterday can be made to produce crops today and that the blood-drenched beaches of Normandy have been washed clean by the waves of the sea. Yes, life's healing power is at work. There is a readiness of natural forces to come to our aid in times of need. One of the leading physicians in America, who has performed hundreds of autopsies, claims that a large proportion of human ills are cured before the victims know they had the affliction.

Alexis Carrel in his book *Man the Unknown* says that "blood carries to each tissue the proper nourishment, but acts, at the same time, as a sewer that takes away the waste products set free by living tissues. It also contains chemical substances and cells capable of repairing organs wherever necessary."

What a wonderful job modern medicine has done and is doing to prolong human life! Yet after medical science has done all that it can, in the final analysis it must rely on life's healing powers to mend the wounds of mankind. As someone has well said, "Man may dress our wounds, but it is God who heals them." This power at work in the world of nature and in the spiritual realm is one and the same power. It is God at work in his world. It is a power that would save us in all areas of life.

Years ago a play appeared entitled *The Man Who Played God*. The title came from the deaf man in the play, who had learned to read people's lips. He lived on the top floor of a high apartment near Central Park in New York City. From this vantage point with a spyglass he watched people on the park benches and by reading their lips could tell what they were saying. To those in trouble he would send down a servant to tell them that their problem was known and help would be sent. When asked where this mysterious kindness came from, the servant replied, "From the man who plays God."

It is sometimes hard for us to imagine things done like that with each of us, but when we think of this healing power reaching out to us constantly through natural channels, it is reasonable to believe that we are connected as individuals with the whole enterprise, and that we are in the care and keeping of a loving God.

MAKING SORROW SERVE

"Blessed are they that mourn: for they shall be comforted."
Matt. 5:4

ALL of us face at one time or another sorrow and suffering. No one welcomes this experience, and surely we feel that there is some sorrow which does not seem to be a blessing. Common sense can hardly discover profit in some tears. To be sorry that we have been caught in some sin brings only remorse. To harbor sorrow which comes from injured pride serves only to embitter.

Yet we know that there is a sorrow which can serve, which brings God's comfort and consolation. Jesus in his second beatitude speaks of such sorrow when he says: "Blessed are they that mourn: for they shall be comforted." What did he mean by this? How can sorrow be made to serve? How can we not simply make the best of it, but how can we make the most of it?

In the first place we know that sorrow can make us better or bitter. Some years ago I was visiting a mother who had lost her daughter. Her sorrow was great, and the years did not heal it. It made her bitter. "Why did God do this to me?" she cried. "There is no justice and love in a God who would do that." Contrast her response to sorrow with that of another mother who faced great loss, but gradually the sorrow which came seemed to serve and make her better. She found truth in Jesus' words. They gave her strength to stand and withstand what life had in store.

In the second place sorrow can serve by adding sympathy

and season to life. There is a mellowness that comes with sorrow that is brought in no other way. Tenderness comes with tears and a capacity for friendship with mourning.

Some years ago following a performance of the Passion play at Oberammergau a visitor spoke to Anton Lang, who played the part of Christus. "When I watched you in the play, it appeared as if the cross were really heavy."

"It is," replied Anton. "I can scarcely lift it."

"Why do you have it so heavy when it is only a play?"

The man playing the part of Christus replied, "If I do not feel the weight, I cannot act the part."

Sorrow helps us feel the weight of other men's troubles. Deep sympathy and mellowness can come with the trail of tears.

And finally sorrow can reveal our helplessness in ourselves and our hopefulness in God. Rather than drive us away from God, it can serve to lead us to him. When sorrow comes, we feel our own helplessness. When we are broken and bruised, then it is so easy for God to come in. Indeed, many times "man's extremity becomes God's opportunity."

To some of you trouble and sorrow has done different things. In some your faith has been shaken, and you have grown cynical and been filled with despair. But others of you have found it to open up the way to life's unfailing resources.

Remember in your sorrow how Jesus said: "My peace I

give unto you: not as the world giveth, give I unto you."
It has been the great sufferers of the world who have
become the great believers. You too can make sorrow
serve in drawing you closer to God. "Blessed are they that
mourn: for they shall be comforted."

WHEN ARE WE FREE?

"Where the Spirit of the Lord is, there is liberty."
                                                    II Cor. 3:17

THERE is no word used more today in our English language than the word "freedom." It falls frequently from the lips of politicians who make their promises to protect the freedom so costly won. It becomes the theme of books as authors deal with this basic desire of human hearts. It finds expression in education and learning, for freedom of quest is essential in the search for knowledge.

Men hate bondage, and in our time the priceless treasures of freedom have gained new attention from those caught under the heels of dictators or from those who fear such slavery.

Jesus, conscious of men's need, declared, "Ye shall know the truth, and the truth shall make you free." He came that men might be free—free from bondage, fear, anxiety. He became man's great liberator. Let us then for a few moments consider the question: When are we free?

In the first place let us see when we are not free. Goethe once said, "None are more hopelessly enslaved than those who falsely believe they are free." Did he not mean that we become enslaved when we falsely believe that we can disregard law?

We can easily see that if we are to move in this world with a measure of freedom, we cannot ignore its laws of physical nature. Let us suppose that a workman would fall from the second floor of one of our large buildings now in process of construction, and that someone rushing up would ask if there was anything he could do and the fallen man would say, "Yes, have the city council suspend the law of gravity until this building is completed." The law of gravity cannot be suspended, and we must respect it if we are to be free.

Huxley once said, "Sit down before facts as a little child, be prepared to give up every preconceived notion, follow humbly wherever and to whatever abyss nature leads, or you shall learn nothing."

No less important nor real are the laws of the moral realm. These, as with the laws of physical nature, cannot be handled lightly. Yet there are some who falsely believe they are free to disregard the sacred vows of marriage and live a lax and loose life. But infidelity exacts its pound of flesh. You cannot have a joyous and happy home and not be true to it.

Yes, we are free to disregard the rights and privileges of others, but that road on the large scale leads to war. Truly "none are more hopelessly enslaved than those who falsely believe they are free."

This leads us to a second consideration, namely, that no one is really free until he is mastered. You have flown a kite and know that, if it is to fly, it must be tied down. It must have a point of anchor, or else it comes down. But with an anchor it is free to roam the heavens. So with a person. If he has a great dream, a great ideal, a great cause to which all of his life is related, then he has a chance at freedom. Paul had this in mind when he said, "Where the Spirit of the Lord is, there is liberty."

In other words, as Epictetus put it, "A man is free only when whatever is the will of God is his will too." Paul found this to be true, and the secret of his emancipated life was that he became mastered by Christ, who liberated him. Herein lies our liberty too.

KEEPING OUR DESIRES HIGH

"Except the Lord build the house, they labour in vain that build it." Ps. 127:1

FOR a long time now we in this modern world have judged the value of a man by what he can do. We have asked, "Can he do the job? Does he know his business?" Industry has been intent in knowing the skills of an employee, whether or not he can produce.

As a result of emphasizing efficiency and competence we have witnessed an amazing civilization, one that has created, has made unbelievable advance in the realm of invention. We have seen far-fetched dreams come true. We have all shared in the benefits of such material progress.

But now we come to this modern scene in despair, for we see that much of our so-called progress was pseudo progress. To be sure, man has with his skills and technique conquered the air with planes, the sea with ships. He has shortened space and to some degree lengthened time with his labor-saving devices. Yet with all his progress man is becoming the victim of that which he has made. The products of man's achievement are turning against him and threatening him. Progress made in the laboratory for the welfare of mankind is turning upon him as some Frankenstein.

Winston Churchill said prophetically in 1924, "Mankind has never been in this position before. Without having improved appreciably in virtue or enjoying wiser guidance, it has got into its hands for the first time the tools by which it can unfailingly accomplish its own extermination."

Now we see it is important not only to be able to do a job, but also to maintain the right desire and purpose in doing it. Technique has outgrown desire; skill has advanced beyond motive; ability to do has gone ahead of quality of wants. We are now witnessing a world of marked advance in skills but of retreat in desires. So we realize that more important than man's ability and efficiency are his goodness, his motive, his purpose in life. We see the dangers of a highly skilled civilization with a low-level motive.

More and more business concerns want to know about the character of a person. It is insufficient to know about the skills of a man unless he can be depended upon. We are coming to see that it is not safe to give into a workman's hands, however skilled they may be, a machine unless that workman has a sense of integrity. It is not safe to turn over a transport plane carrying cargoes of human life to a skilled pilot if that pilot cannot be depended upon to stay sober. Nor can the achievements of scientific invention be left unchecked in the hands of ruthless men. The laboratory is not safe for mankind unless those who have it at their disposal have desires which are good. "Power," said Alfred the Great, "is never a good unless he be good that has it."

How can we keep our desires and wants high and noble? There is only one answer. Only as men give their allegiance to God through Christ can they be safe in risking their desires and the desires of other men. The world will be at peace only when its dominant desire becomes Christian.

THE OVERFLOW OF GOD'S LOVE

*"The Lord is my shepherd; I shall not want. . . . My cup
runneth over."* Ps. 23:1, 5

THE closer we live to God, the more we see that
his love and goodness to us are boundless. The more our
lives are spent in adoration, the more we see for us to
enjoy. God has so richly dressed this world that reflecting
upon his graciousness overwhelms us.

Oftentimes living so close to work which may have
become a drudgery, staying close by a radio for the latest
news, reflecting continually upon life's tragedies—all this
can make us miss seeing the wonder and majesty of God's
love, always evident to those with eyes that see. If we
get too close to a tree, our view of what lies beyond may be
obliterated. One tree may shut from our gaze a forest. One
tragedy may prevent us from seeing beyond to its use. One
war may eclipse for us all that is good within the world.
One failure of a friend may blot from our memory all
remembrance of good deeds done. Yes, we need to ascend
to a steeple to gain an accurate view of a town.

The Psalmist knew of this overflow of God's love when
he said, "The Lord is my shepherd; I shall not want,"
and, "My cup runneth over." No wonder this expression of
faith and thanksgiving has become a favorite, for in their
better moments people find in these immortal words expression of their own experiences and deeper feelings. Indeed
God's love does overflow!

Look at his world. He has not skimped in making this

world lovely. Merton Rice has said, "God's hand is forever outreaching the dictates of necessity." He has filled the world with all sorts of extras in making grass green, skies blue, and sunsets orange and red. Even the horror of war cannot erase nature's loveliness. Battle-scarred fields within a few months turn from parched earth to green rolling hills and flowering valleys.

God could have so easily clothed his earth with garments not pleasing to the eye. His skies could have become ugly reflections in pools of water rather than lustrous blue. His pure air could have contained unpleasant odors which stifle rather than that which invigorates.

His world is not bad except where men have made it bad. His world is not evil except where the greed of men has spoiled it. This is our Father's world, and his creation is good. Even the impulses of men so often leading to ways of destruction were meant to be used for lovely purposes. The heated passions of men if abused can lead to hell, but if controlled and rightly used point the way to heaven. Turning unto God we find the meaning of life. Outside his hands life is filled with terror and tragedy. Within his hands life is filled with purpose and abiding joy. A God who cares like that is one who surely inspired the Psalmist to sing, "My cup runneth over."

KINDNESS WARMS THE HEART

"Take care that none of you ever pays back evil for evil, but always try to treat one another and everybody with kindness."   I Thess. 5:15 (Goodspeed)

SOMETIMES we wonder if what we are doing is worth while and if we really are needed. Then all of a sudden some kind, thoughtful soul passes our way and gives us new faith. He thanks us for what we have done or what we are doing. He seems to feel that our last visit, the recent letter, the short talk, the stand we took—such made a difference to him. What would we do without our friends who believe in us and once in a while let us know it?

We go home at night and childish voices express their joy in having us home again. A wife depends on us; a child looks to us; a husband finds encouragement in us; a brother, a sister—in spite of childish differences—loves us. When the day has been hard, when cares have pushed in upon us, when mistakes have faced us—how a kind word warms our hearts and makes us feel we are needed after all!

Many times I think of the faith and new hope which the wife of Nathaniel Hawthorne gave him. You recall how after losing a job he comes home brokenhearted and in great despair. But he is met by his wife with a faith that quickens his ebbing hope. Now she says he can write that book which he has always wanted to write and which she knows he can write. To clinch the matter she shows him money she's saved over the years for this moment. She has saved enough to see him through. Propelled by her faith he begins and gives to the world one of America's greatest novels, *The Scarlet Letter*. In gratitude for this faith Nathaniel writes to Sophia, his wife:

Thou only hast taught me that I have a heart—thou only hast thrown a light downward and upward into my soul. Thou only hast revealed me to myself; for without thy aid my best knowledge of myself would have been merely to know my own shadow—to watch it flickering on the wall and mistake its fantasies for my own real actions.

If more wives and husbands today had faith such as that in each other, divorces would decrease and little children would find security in the love their parents had for each other.

But beyond our human affection and love we need to feel and know that love which is at the heart of life, for greater than the faith men have in us is God's faith in us. He gives us the benefit of the doubt. He is ever ready to give us a new chance, a new lease on life. He takes us with bad pasts, with miserable failures, with scarred records, and believes in what we may become.

We need to seal and strengthen our human affections with his affection. Theodore Adams tells the story of a young woman whose husband was in service in Japan. He sent her a treasured picture of himself. The unique thing about the picture was the signature. Rather than signing his name the young man had written a few musical notes at the bottom. In explanation she said: "My husband was sent to Japan on special duty just a short time after we were married. He had this picture made and sent it to me. I was puzzled about the signature too and wrote to ask him what it meant. He replied, 'It comes from the song "Because."' I went through the song until I found just the right notes, and the signature really says, 'And pray his love may make our love divine.'"

TRUE RELIGION GENERATES LIGHT

"Thou shalt love the Lord thy God with all thy heart, and with all thy soul, and with all thy mind."　　Matt. 23:37

ON ONE occasion when Jesus was asked to name the first and great commandment, he answered by quoting an ancient Jewish rule: "Thou shalt love the Lord thy God with all thy heart, and with all thy soul, and with all thy mind." How important it is in these days of tension and confusion to listen especially to the latter part of Jesus' injunction, "with all thy mind"! We are called upon to love God not only with our heart but also with our mind. Someone has said, "It is not enough to say of a person that his heart is in the right place if his head and hands are in the wrong place."

Of course we all recognize the place emotion has in life. It plays a vital role in our faith, for a religion without emotion and deep feeling is a waterless sort of thing without much real life.

But saying all this and no more leaves us with only a half-truth. Men must be not just impelled to act or move, but also given purpose and direction in that action. This all boils down to the fact that religion concerns the mind as well as the heart. It deals with thought as well as feeling. One of the profoundest needs of our time is for dedicated minds.

The Church has always recognized that true religion generates light as well as heat. This need for brains in religion, this interest in light as well as zeal was brought to a focus by Paul when in writing to the Romans he said, "I bear them witness that they have a zeal for God, but not according to knowledge."

Our Lord was looked upon as a learned person. He was said to be a man of great wisdom, although he had never been schooled by the accepted standards of the day. He was saluted by wise men as Rabbi or Master, which is the modern equivalent of Doctor or Professor. He was a scholarly man.

We need not fear the truth today. Jesus said, "Ye shall know the truth, and the truth shall make you free." There is no conflict between any new discovery or any truth and our faith. For the same God who reveals himself in our Bible is the same God who permits the uncovering of his truth in the laboratory. There is no conflict between science and religion.

The Christian Church has always been vitally concerned with the spread of knowledge, has considered it a solemn obligation to foster schools of learning to enlighten the mind. It believes that true religion generates light as well as heat. It was Christianity which during the Dark Ages kept the lamp of learning aglow.

Give your hearts to God. No one who knows anything about life and religion would depreciate the importance of the emotional life. It is our driving power. Also give your heads to God. He needs warm hearts and dedicated minds at work in his kingdom. He needs all of us to "worship him in spirit and in truth."

THE RISK OF FAITH

"Faith is the substance of things hoped for, the evidence of things not seen."   Heb. 11:1

PAUL says that "faith is the substance of things hoped for, the evidence of things not seen." He is saying in effect that faith is always a risk, for the reality of the evidence does not fully come until one has plunged in. First we believe, we trust, and then we find our trust has been vindicated. The evidence of those things not seen comes to us when we live as if we saw them.

This sounds like a strange paradox—to believe something you cannot see in order to see it. Yet it is not so strange when we realize that much of life is based on this truth. There are many experiences in life which cannot be completely understood until those experiences are entered into.

Let us take love for an example. It is the sort of experience which has to be entered into if we are to know its real meaning. To be sure, we can see how it affects two people. We can watch their devotion to each other, their fidelity and deep concern. But we cannot know what it means until we love and are loved. We can imagine what concern a parent has for a child when we witness the sacrifices that are made that the child may have a chance in life. But we can never fully know that concern until we hold our own child in our arms. We may offer our sympathy as best we can to one who has lost a lifelong companion, one who has shared as husband or wife life's joys and sorrows. But we can never know the anguish of separation and the long night watches, when sleep will not come, until we have passed that way.

Charles Clayton Morrison has well said, "Every act of faith involves a hazard. Faith is not mere belief in evidence. It is putting to the test of conduct a course of living for which no absolute proof can be found short of the actual experience of living that way." Trying to interpret the Christian experience from the outside is like seeing a cathedral window from the streets. Only as we go inside and look out against the daylight can the beauty of color and form of the window really be seen.

So our faith in the reality and reliability of God in Christ can find its complete proof only in experience. To find him men oftentimes must live as if there is a God and then God will reveal himself. Donald Hankey said the same in this way: "Faith is betting your life that there is a God." Another, named Pascal, expressed it thus: "We must wager." The writer to the Hebrews says this: "For he that cometh to God must believe that he is, and that he is a rewarder of them that diligently seek him."

Our faith in God through Christ does not depend upon our belief in certain credentials which claim to support his divinity. No, our real faith in him comes from the evidence gained in our trust in him and our experience of him. As we trust him along the way, new evidences of all sorts spring up to support and vindicate our faith.

Do we learn to swim by reading the instruction book or listening to lectures of a lifeguard? No, we plunge in.

Likewise with our faith. We take the plunge, and if we are faithful in our efforts and trustful in our living, we experience such fruits that convince us of the reality of Christ and his way.

Perchance there is someone reading this today who desperately feels the need for his peace and power and love and yet who is waiting for further evidence. Plunge in, my friend. Although his love and mercy sound too good to be true, your risk will vindicate itself.

OUR LIVES ARE LIKE MIRRORS

"As he thinketh in his heart, so is he."   Prov. 23:7

BERNARD IDDINGS BELL says that the disciples "were men of common clay. They were unlearned. When they started the Christian life, they were dull, faithless, hesitant, reluctant, cowardly as many of us today. But look what they became . . . lovers of mankind." And the thing which changed them is what can change you and me.

We become like that upon which we habitually gaze. Formation of brave, sturdy character is no mystery. The brave soul is one who has through the years gazed on bravery. The lovely spirit has grown like that by looking upon loveliness. You tell me what you look at in your mind and heart, and I will tell you what you will become. Our lives in reality are like mirrors reflecting in ourselves what we continually gaze upon.

A. N. Whitehead in his book *The Aims of Education* says that "moral education is impossible without the habitual vision of greatness." Commenting on this, Richard Livingstone has pointed out that

No one achieves greatness in any field or activity unless he habitually gazes with reverent admiration upon the best achievements in that field. No musician becomes great whose habitual contemplation is not the best in music; no poet becomes great who is not habitually bathing his soul in the best there is of poetry; no architect unless he is familiar with the great examples of art.

OUR LIVES ARE LIKE MIRRORS

We become like that with which we linger. Linger in the presence of the cheap, the small, the vulgar, and you partake of it. Gaze habitually on the great, the magnanimous, the lovely, and you become like it. In this highest of all arts, the art of living as a human being, achievement in that is impossible without habitual vision of greatness. "The sense that men make out of life," says Dean Wicks, "is determined by what claims their deepest attention."

In our search for something to gaze upon we are restless and torn until we find God, who gives us a vision of what is great and of what makes life worth while. Never are we completely satisfied with that upon which we set our attention; restless we are until we find our rest in him. God has placed within our reach a vision of himself, and we find that in Christ. Gazing on him we gaze on God. "He that hath seen me hath seen the Father."

To gaze habitually on him gives us the finest of companionship. All of us are constantly being made by the companions we keep. We cannot escape the influence of companions, but we can choose the company we keep.

In a little village in Europe where rose perfume is manufactured girls leaving the factory in the late afternoon carry with them the odor of perfume. The scent of roses clings to their garments even after they leave their workrooms. So it is with life and with Christ. Live with him long enough and his thoughts become our thoughts, his desires become our desires, and his dreams become our dreams. Lost in his greatness we partake of it.

HANDLING OUR FEARS

"There is no fear in love; but perfect love casteth out fear."
                                        I John 4:18

ALL of us face fear in one form or another. Aristotle once said that a man "would deserve to be called insane or insensible if there were nothing that he feared, not even an earthquake or a storm at sea."

There are financial fears—anxiety over the job or the meager income, trying to make ends meet, wondering if we please our bosses and whether or not our jobs are permanent. We have fears of ill health. Many prospective brides and grooms are haunted before marriage (and sometimes afterward) by the fear of having chosen the wrong partner.

Yet fear is not always a villain. On the contrary it may be a benevolent force making us aware of physical dangers. It can be a red-light signal, a "stop, look, listen" sign of impending doom. Fear keeps us from being hit by a train. It discourages us from living in unsanitary conditions, from disobeying the doctor's orders. In a sense we are blessed by the capacity to know fear.

But there is a difference between desirable and undesirable fear. A little is necessary, but excessive amounts distort our whole future. Therefore our business in one sense is not to get rid of fear but to harness it, to curb it, to master it, to learn to handle it. How then are we to handle fear?

In the first place our fears should be faced. We should

drag them into the open and see them as they really are. We should look at them in the light of day. What is their origin? Where did they come from? Is my fear real or imaginary? Getting it out into the open is of utmost importance. Many times we discover that those fears which haunted us are ungrounded. Facing our fears, staring them in the face, trying to run them down to their source, sometimes leads to their disappearance.

A second suggestion is that our fears should be met with action. Abraham Myerson, a psychologist, strongly insists on action even if it is unwise action, for such is better than living under the fear which tends to breed another fear. Brooding is the worst thing we can do.

By action is also meant that it is good to do the thing you fear. If you fear ill health, go to a doctor. If you dread loneliness, share another's suffering. If you fear to be around certain people, deliberately go around them. Many times doing the thing we fear helps to conquer it.

Finally remember we face our fears not alone. All of us have experienced the added strength and courage a companion gives when we are on a strange and dangerous journey. We know what it is to have someone standing by when we face sorrow and suffering. It is wonderful what the presence of a friend will do to help dispel the gloom and restore new confidence.

But greater than all human companionship, some of which may be fickle and in time prove faithless, is a divine companionship, the great companionship—the companionship of the Christ. Multitudes of people the world over have found in Jesus Christ one who calms their fears and restores their hopes. Believing in him, trusting in his power, and accepting him as Lord and Master of life drive out men's fears and make brave hearts.

THE HAPPY HEART

"These things have I spoken unto you, that my joy might remain in you, and that your joy might be full." John 15:11

OVER the stage of a social hall of a church in which I once served are written these words: "A merry heart doeth good like a medicine." These words are found in the seventeenth chapter of Proverbs, the twenty-second verse, and are words which we need to take to heart today.

We all know that they are true. A man happy in his work discovers a tonic for his health. A person who keeps a joyous outlook finds a healing medicine. With joy goes health.

Conversely worry and misery bring bad health. Modern medicine knows that it is not enough to treat a disease but a patient, a person. No longer do wise doctors think only in terms of an appendectomy but of a person who has a bad appendix that must come out. The whole person must be treated, for the outlook of a patient is directly related to recovery.

All of us then must be interested in maintaining a happy outlook and a joyous heart. The question is where to find such—and how to maintain a happy heart independent of the rise and fall of circumstances.

If we turn to Jesus for our answer, we will find that our Lord was a man of great joy. To be sure, he has been represented as a man of sorrows and one acquainted with grief. Certainly he knew sorrow and grief. He felt and feels deeply today about human suffering. But overshadowing his grief was a radiant joy which was contagious.

Little children sought his presence. Old men came in the dead of night. He was invited to a marriage feast to make merry. To the man lying on his bed sick with palsy he said, "Be of good cheer."

Wherever you turn in the New Testament, you find words of hope and of joy. It is indeed the most joyous book in the world. It opens with the joy of birth and ends with the multitude singing the Hallelujah Chorus. Wherever you turn, there is the note of gladness.

At his farewell supper Jesus said, "These things have I spoken unto you, that my joy might remain in you, and that your joy might be full." So, Christianity is the most joyous religion in the world. Let us then see what was the secret of Jesus' joy. What were some of its deep sources?

In the first place his joy came out of a conviction that he was helping and not hurting men. He was conscious that he was doing a great and abiding service to men. He was always giving—healing the blind, making the lame to walk, comforting the brokenhearted.

But most of us begin life seeking joy through getting and have to learn that the deepest satisfaction comes through serving. There is a universal law that the happiest people on earth are those doing the most for others.

Can you remember the joy which was yours in doing some abiding service for a person who had no special reason to expect it from you? The Chinese have this to say about such:

"A bit of fragrance always clings to the hand that gives the roses." So Jesus' joy came from finding lost and needy people and helping them.

In the second place his joy came from a conviction that he was doing right. He had a strong assurance that he was doing the will of his heavenly Father. There was the sense of God's approval on his life. This is the kind of assurance we need if we would maintain abiding joy.

Edwin Lewis has said, "Nothing gives a man stability like a conviction that what he is doing is right."

Ralph W. Sockman says, "Many people have enough religion to make them feel uncomfortable when they do wrong, but not enough to make them feel good when they do right."

And finally his joy came from a conviction of hope based on his faith that God can be trusted. For him there was nothing too good to believe about God. He had a joyous idea of God—a Father who valued men's souls, one to whom he could go any time.

He saw God everywhere, in lilies of the field, songs of the birds, laughter of children, and confidently believed that God's presence was with him. He was a God who numbered the hairs of one's head.

It was on such trust that Jesus' joy was based. So we can see that the sources of his joy were not at the mercy of men or circumstances. He lived a life of joy in spite of what life did to him. He offers us that same joy through faith in him and his way.

THROUGH THE STORM

"All things work together for good to them that love God."

Rom. 8:28

MOST of us have sung these words of a hymn:

> Jesus calls us, o'er the tumult
> Of our life's wild, restless sea;
> Day by day His sweet voice soundeth,
> Saying, "Christian, follow me."

What do we mean when we say "Jesus calls us"? Of course the full meaning of his call is beyond the complete understanding of our minds, and, too, it may have varying implications for different persons. But among its many meanings let us consider one today.

Jesus calls us from a faith dependent upon the rise and fall of circumstances to one rooted and grounded in God's love.

To be sure, we cannot escape the effect of circumstances or the way we feel and the way we look at life. Environment and circumstances do color our living. But our Lord offers us a faith with resources which makes us joyous even when the tide of circumstances turns against us. Else how do we explain Bunyan's *Pilgrim's Progress,* written while he lay twelve years in Bedford's jail? Or how do we explain the radiant witness of Peter when faced with the angry temple authorities after healing the lame man? He said, "Whether it be right in the sight of God to hearken unto you more than unto God, judge ye. For we cannot but speak the things which we have seen and heard."

Yes, when one's faith is rooted and grounded in God's love, he is assured that "all things work together for good to them that love God." All of us have been through days when we found it hard to believe that all things work together for good, but when we add "to them that love God," it takes on different meaning.

Ralph W. Sockman gives us the analogy of a ship. He says:

There are parts of a ship which left to themselves would sink. The engine, the shafts, the steel girders—all these, if taken out of a ship, would settle to the bottom of the sea. But when those heavy steel parts are built into the frame of a ship, the ship floats. So it is with life. That wound of a friend, that business failure, that son's death—such sorrows taken singly would sink us; but when these are fitted into the framework of life whose builder and maker is God, they keep it afloat. Yes, all things, good and bad, can be carried on the voyage of life if we keep our love and trust in the goodness of God.[1]

I am certain that our Lord offers us an inner sense of peace and satisfaction which the world cannot take away. It is a serenity that draws strength from the hidden springs of the spirit. If we have missed this calm confidence which makes for genuine happiness, we have missed much of the Christian faith.

[1] From *Now to Live!* Copyright 1946 by Stone & Pierce.

Real faith in Christ is a faith that cannot be shaken by the misfortunes of daily living. As Christians we are to expect hardships and trials and tribulations, but our faith is not to be shaken by them.

Remember the courage and undaunted faith of those three men Shadrach, Meshach, and Abednego. As they faced the fiery furnace, they said to the king: "If it be so, our God whom we serve is able to deliver us from the burning fiery furnace, and he will deliver us out of thine hand, O king. But if not, be it known unto thee, O king, that we will not serve thy gods, nor worship the golden image which thou hast set up." Remember also the words of our Lord when he cried out, "If it be possible, let this cup pass from me: nevertheless not as I will, but as thou wilt." Such a faith is rooted and grounded in the love of God.

Robert Louis Stevenson was on a voyage to the South Seas when a terrific storm arose. The passengers were huddled together, frightened. One man made his way to the bridge and saw the captain pacing there. After watching him for a while he returned to his fellow passengers. They asked him fearfully what he had learned and what their chances were. He replied, "I have seen the captain's face and all is well." To know Jesus and to accept his call is to have faith that all is well, whatever may happen. The glory of our faith is that even if we do face suffering and sorrow, we have the assurance of resources and power which Christ gives that will see us through the storm. Jesus calls us to this kind of faith.

GROWING UP SPIRITUALLY

"And Jesus increased in wisdom and stature, and in favour with God and man."   Luke 2:52

WE KNOW what it means to grow up physically. Evidences of it are easy to see, such as added weight and increased height. Likewise we understand growth intellectually. It is marked by our increased interest in and understanding of life and its mysteries.

Psychologists have developed a system of measuring the intellectual growth of a person. They call such a rating one's Intelligence Quotient or I.Q. for short. The I.Q. rating is an indication of capacity to learn and the achievement in learning.

But when we come to spiritual growth, we do not find the marks so easily distinguished. If we had such a measurement that would rate a person's spiritual growth, an S.Q. say, it might surprise many a man with a splendid intellectual development to discover that his Spiritual Quotient was not so splendid. Many a man is more concerned with physical and intellectual growth than with spiritual, and yet it is a person's spiritual capacity and development that gives meaning to the whole man.

Truly, attaining spiritual maturity is a lifetime matter. We never fully arrive. Our goal is an ever-receding one. Such growth is a pilgrimage. It is a journey. It is one in which we can never rest but must always be on the march. Indeed, becoming a Christian is to start on a journey in learning to apply this new-found light to the days of our years.

What are some of the marks of those who have followed that road? What are some characteristics of a spiritually mature person?

First, to be spiritually mature is to face trouble with confidence. Such a one knows that he is not facing his trouble alone, but with an ally God. Such a one is the man who prayed each day: "O Lord, help me to remember that nothing is going to happen to me today that you and I cannot handle."

Of course one does not gain such confidence overnight. It comes with spiritual growth and is the thing that makes spiritual growth worth while. Some of the most radiant people are those who in spite of trouble have found strength where they are.

In the second place, to be spiritually mature is to maintain a sense of humor. Indeed, to be able to laugh at oneself is a mark of spiritual growth. Does this sound strange? Levity is not lightness. It is maintaining top anchorage. Most of us take ourselves too seriously. But to be able to laugh in the midst of difficulty can often ease the strain and clear the vision.

To be mature spiritually is to enjoy the very process of life—living. It is to find meaning not only in life's goals toward which we labor but also in the actual journey we travel in reaching those goals. It is to enjoy our work and not merely the fruits of our work—to enjoy the plowing, the sowing, as well as the garnering in.

Again, when one's Spiritual Quotient is high, he is able to meet criticism with intelligence. The real mark of a man is the size of the thing it takes to get his goat. To be sure, we should be concerned with what others say and think, but not too concerned. Many remarks were never intended as criticism, and yet we let them wound us.

But when a criticism is just, why not be grateful and profit from it by correcting our ways? The spiritually mature will never worry about words which were intended only to hurt, for they know that truth takes care of itself.

Finally, to be mature spiritually is to live as if every day were the only day. Whatever one is doing, if it is honorable and good, if it is done well, let him not be fearful if, while doing it, life comes to an end. Live with confidence, knowing that all things work together for good to them that love God, for to love God truly is to be spiritually mature.

THE SECRET OF AN UNTROUBLED HEART

"Wait on the Lord: be of good courage, and he shall strengthen thine heart: wait, I say, on the Lord."   Ps. 27:14

IT IS clearer to me now than ever before that millions of people today are living with troubled hearts. It seems that so many have come my way, distressed and filled with futility.

One person said, "Look at the front page of our daily newspapers. What you see there is within itself enough to give us troubled hearts."

Indeed, no man knows what the future holds, but certainly every thoughtful person believes that we are destined to live the remainder of our lives in tension and turmoil.

Elton Trueblood has reminded us that instead of pining for calmer days the way of wisdom is to learn to live realistically in such a time of strain.

Certainly I am not bold enough to say that I know how to live with a sense of inner peace nor that I can tell you in 1, 2, 3, 4, how to keep an untroubled heart. But we do find comfort in Jesus' words, a clue to our need, in the fourteenth chapter of John, twenty-seventh verse, where he says, "Peace I leave with you, my peace I give unto you: not as the world giveth, give I unto you. Let not your heart be troubled, neither let it be afraid."

Let us explore this secret of an untroubled heart, of how to live with a sense of inner calm in the presence of a storm.

In the first place an untroubled heart comes with the

assurance that what we are doing is right. There is no satisfaction in life to be compared with the conviction that what we are doing is right, that the side we are on is God's side. To do things that we know deep down we should not do may for a moment bring a sense of exultation, but sooner or later a hang-over will come. To live in conscious dread of failing to measure up to what is expected, of being proved guilty, of knowing that we have committed a deed unworthy of our name and heritage—such fear can tear upon our inward parts and sap energies needed for labor and service.

You and I cannot maintain an untroubled heart unless we gain the inner satisfaction that comes with the conviction that what we are doing is right. We cannot do wrong and still feel right.

In the second place it helps us to have an untroubled heart when we accept the fact that we cannot carry all the world's load on our own shoulders.

This does not mean that we are to shirk our responsibilities nor blind our eyes to the crying needs the world over. It does not mean that we are to grow callous to human need. But it does mean that there are some problems over which we have absolutely no control. It does mean that there are some things in life that future generations must answer for themselves.

Anne Lindbergh in her book *North to the Orient* says, "We must not exceed our limited weight budget." She tells of the careful sorting and resorting of the articles the Lindberghs would carry on a trip until they got down to absolute essentials.

Well might we learn to do this in life, to sort out our mental baggage and rid ourselves of nonessentials—to know the difference between that over which we have no control and which we do control.

And finally, when Jesus said, "Let not your heart be troubled, neither let it be afraid," he was speaking surely of that assurance which can be ours that the trouble we bear is not carried alone.

An old lady was carrying a heavy grip and just managed to catch her train before it moved out of the station. Standing in the aisle, she still held her grip, until the conductor, noticing, said, "You can put it down now, lady. The train will carry it for you."

Most of us carry unnecessary loads. "Cast thy burden upon the Lord, and he shall sustain thee." The Psalmist knew of the help the Lord gives when he wrote: "I waited patiently for the Lord; and he inclined unto me, and heard my cry. He brought me up also out of an horrible pit, out of the miry clay, and set my feet upon a rock, and established my goings. And he hath put a new song in my mouth, even praise unto our God."

OUR REFUGE AND STRENGTH

"God is our refuge and strength, a very present help in trouble."   Ps. 46:1

A LITTLE girl in a certain southern city was describing to her friend the location of the church she was attending. She said, "It is the church down the street that has a plus mark on top."

What a wonderful way to describe a church, for surely the cross represents a plus mark in life! And what a marvelous way to describe a Christian as being a person who has a plus quality about him!

Jesus was thinking of this difference when in the Sermon on the Mount he said, "For if ye love them which love you, what reward have ye? do not even the publicans the same? And if ye salute your brethren only, what do ye more than others? do not even the publicans so?"

This phrase "what do ye more than others?" suggests to us that there should be something different about the Christian. There should be a certain radiance about his life that sets him off from those who do not profess Christianity.

In the first place Christ makes a difference, for in him we find a strength that helps us stand the loads of life. I believe with all my heart that beyond our fondest imaginations and expectations, when the unwanted comes upon us, ready for use are resources from the hand of God that will enable us to see it through.

God does not grant us any experience in life without offering resources to help us see it through. Not long ago a person faced with a tragic experience and with a future that seemed to many so very hopeless said this to me: "You know, if someone had told me before this happened that I could have stood it, I would not have believed it." This good woman was discovering what it meant to place oneself in the hands of God, to believe what he said when he promised, "Come unto me, all ye that labour and are heavy laden, and I will give you rest."

Although God does not save us from trouble, we do know that he saves us in trouble. In him is strength that helps us stand the loads of life.

Again we find in Christ the strength that helps us stand the temptations of life. He not only gives us the insight and a sensitive conscience to see our duty, but offers us the power to see it through.

In Lloyd Douglas' book *The Robe* Justus is talking to Marcellus. Justus says, "I only know that he is alive. . . . Sometimes I feel aware of him, as if he were close by. . . . It keeps you honest. . . . You have no temptation to cheat anyone, or lie to anyone, or hurt anyone—when, for all you know, Jesus is standing beside you."

Marcellus says that such would make him very uncomfortable. Then Justus replies, "Not if that presence helped you defend yourself against yourself. . . . It is a great satisfaction to have someone standing by—to keep you at your best." [1]

[1] Used by permission of the publishers, Houghton Mifflin Co.

Certainly if anyone should have been discouraged by the failures and faults of men, it would have been Jesus. Although he was betrayed and denied and crucified, yet he had such a love and respect for men that he said as he hung upon the cross, "Father, forgive them; for they know not what they do."

Contrast his view of men with those who discount the value of human beings. There are cynics who say that man is merely a sick fly on a dizzy wheel. Materialists would have us believe that we are only a bundle of electrons with no soul. Some would-be psychologists, certainly not Christian, say that man is a jumble of stimuli-response-reactions with no enduring value.

But over against such disparagement of human nature we come face to face with the Christian conception of man. No other interpretation is so satisfying. We are children of God. We are creatures of infinite worth because we are important to God. Jesus sought through comparison to give us some idea of God's love for us. "If ye . . . know how to give good gifts unto your children, how much more shall your Father which is in heaven?" Yes, if parents will sacrifice for their children, how much more God? If a man will lay down his life for his friend, how much more God?

Lacordaire once dramatized this truth of God's love when he said, "If you would wish to know how the Almighty feels toward us, listen to the beating of your own heart and add to it infinity."

Here was the Master on board a vessel when a fierce

storm arose and the disciples were afraid. Then you remember he came on deck and said, not only to the heaving waves but to the distressed disciples, "Peace, be still." He calmed their fears.

This confidence comes to us today from the realization that we worship a living Lord and not a dead one. Leslie Weatherhead has this to say in his book *When the Lamp Flickers:* "Jesus does not wave to us from the past; he beckons us from the future."

He is alive, here and now, moving and working among men. Confidence, then, comes to us when we know that we labor and live and love and laugh not alone. He is always standing by.

So today amid the strain and stress of our daily living we find our Lord, if we but let him, calming our fears and making us know that "God is our refuge and strength, a very present help in trouble." This is the difference that Christ makes.

A VOICE FROM ON HIGH

"The Word was made flesh, and dwelt among us."

John 1:14

AMONG the personal effects of a serviceman killed in the South Pacific was a notebook in which he had written these words:

This is the time for a new revelation. People don't think much about religion nowadays. But we need a voice from on high, brother, and I don't mean maybe. This thing has gotten out of human ability to run. I'm no religious fanatic. But we are in a situation where something better than human brains has got to give us advice.

His words are but the symbol of the feeling of millions today the world over who have come to believe that our only hope rests in some power beyond man, that can lead us out of this terrible time of confusion. No one who looks into the faces of men today can escape seeing mirrored there heartache, anxiety, fear, sorrow. Men are heavy-laden, tempest-tossed, time-torn, fear-filled, today. The strains of this modern world take terrific toll. Uncertainties dampen many spirits. Heavy loads break many backs. Deep-seated sin lurks in many hearts and crucifies many souls.

George C. Marshall was thinking of this when he said that the most important thing for the world today is spiritual regeneration.

Indeed men are confused today and want a sure word.

Voices from every side are beckoning for attention. "Come follow me. Here is the way out. We have the answer." Materialism has said, "Create more things. Invent more gadgets. Discover more machines. Science is the way out." But men find in science that which unchecked leads to destruction. Science in the hands of ruthless men offers no hope. Dictatorship has said, "Give power into my hands, and I will bring order and peace. Drop every allegiance, and give me your loyalty. I will simplify life and give you the way out." But dictatorship has taken power in our time and turned it to evil uses.

Like a station master announcing departing trains, going in all directions, we hear a jumble of voices offering solution to our confusion. Our lives are embattled shores bombarded from many guns. Many would-be masters lure us on.

Gerald Kennedy expressed such this way:

We find ourselves with tremendous powers of communication, but no healing word to speak; tremendous systems of transportation, but nothing to transport that will make life whole again; tremendous powers of production, but no knowledge of how to produce the kind of life that will keep us from committing suicide. . . .

It is all right to think of the world as a stage and each man playing his part, but there comes a time when we must ask ourselves who wrote the play. What kind of drama is it? And how is it going to end? Shall we think of the conclusion of the whole business as a whining farce, or as a triumphant tragedy? No man who considers his life, and, as Plato said, the unconsidered life is not worth living, does so without being driven to religion.[1]

Men today want a sure word. Men want to know what is authentic. Men follow what seems at the time to offer the greatest satisfaction. But the tragedy is that false masters offer only temporary satisfaction. Their glitter is that of the five- and ten-cent store—imitation. It tarnishes overnight.

But God has the answer to men's confusion by giving us a sure word in Christ. We read in John's Gospel, "And the Word was made flesh, and dwelt among us." His way is the only way. His offer is the only offer which is sure. Following him becomes the only wise course. The truth, the light, the hope, the way became known in him when God made him flesh, to dwell among men.

So if you would have a sure word, you find your answer in Christ. If you would be freed from confusion, you find your course in him. Augustine was right when he penned long ago that our souls are restless until they find their rest in God.

[1] From *His Word Through Preaching*. Used by permission of the publishers, Harper & Brothers.

POSSESSIONS WORTHY TO BE SHARED

"There is a lad here, which hath five barley loaves, and two small fishes: but what are they among so many?" John 6:9

ONE day I read a statement which is packed with truth: "God can use an ordinary fellow to do extraordinary things."

How true this is when applied to history. Here is a boy with a few loaves of bread and a few fishes. With them God fed a multitude. Here is a gardener's son in Scotland who became the discoverer of penicillin. Here is a baby born in a one-room log house with only one door, one window, and a dirt floor; and yet God made out of him the greatest man America has produced. Hodgenville, Kentucky, will always be remembered as the birthplace of Abraham Lincoln.

It is amazing to see what those who seem to have so little give when God becomes their partner. Our real value to society consists not in the amount of wealth we can accumulate but in what we have which can be shared with others. These are the things which when shared we often still keep, and oftentimes the more we share, the more we keep for ourselves.

Physical possessions of course are acceptable, but even their value is determined by the spirit in which they are shared. Bread is desperately needed in our world today, but if in giving it a Shylock's repayment is asked in return, it had better not be given. Daisies given in affection by a little child to its mother are of greater significance than orchids just given. Physical possessions when given diminish in quantity, but there are others which when shared increase. They are life's genuine sharable gifts. They deal with spiritual and mental possessions.

What are some of these possessions? For one thing, how the open courage of one person can quicken the hidden courage of another! The courage to make the best of un-ideal situations is worthily sharable.

This is true on a battlefield as a general leads his army to victory with no thought of his own safety. All the great battles of life have been won not on fields of battle, but in communities like our own, when human beings stand, even beyond expected endurance.

Who of us have not profited by such courage? Here is a wife nursing her beloved husband who has no chance of recovery. Yet she stands by with little children in the midst of heavy strains and does so with quiet confidence. How many mothers and wives looking on have had their courage quickened by the open courage of this good woman?

Here is a woman facing life with no hope of good health, but facing it with tranquillity of spirit. Here is a little boy caught by a crippling disease learning to walk again. Here is another purple heart, on the home front, who with meager income sustains a family left broken and penniless by a shiftless father. Courage like this is a possession worthy of being shared.

Then there is a moral courage in the face of opposition which inspires us. We are told that John Stuart Mill once passed severe criticism upon certain classes in England.

It seems that the newspapers did not present his position in the most favorable light, and he was assailed bitterly by those who demanded an explanation. He appeared one day at a political meeting and faced an angry mob ready to do him physical harm. Then he stepped to the front of the platform and said: "You want to know if I said this—well, I did." There was a moment of awkward silence, and then the crowd broke into applause. They became his friends. They were inspired by his moral courage.

Savonarola, the great preacher of Florence, during the reign of Lorenzo the Magnificent criticized the administration. It brought down the wrath of Lorenzo, who threatened the priest with his life. They became bitter enemies. But when Lorenzo lay dying, he sent for Savonarola. "He was the only priest who ever dared to differ with me," said the ruler. Deep down he admired such moral courage.

So it has been in your life and mine: when some brave spirit has stood up for what is right against strong opposition, it has served to strengthen our courage and to help us stand when we might have fallen.

Indeed, this is a possession worth sharing with others.

AT CHRISTMASTIME

"No room . . . in the inn."   Luke 2:7

AT CHRISTMASTIME our minds go back to that manger scene where the Christ child lay and how crowded conditions in Bethlehem forced Joseph to take his wife to a stable where she was to give birth to her first-born son.

We can imagine the great sense of concern which must have been Joseph's and the anxiety of Mary in being crowded out of the inn. In these days of housing shortages and crowded hotel conditions, especially in large cities, we can appreciate the uneasiness that gripped Joseph. Parents of young children are turned away by apartment owners who want couples without children as renters.

But the point of my story is not merely to refresh our memories with the fact that there was no room in Bethlehem, but to call attention to the fact that there is still far too little room for Christ in modern life, and that in many areas of our living today there is standing room only.

The ancient hotelkeeper may have been the first to refuse him room, but unfortunately he has not been the last. To be sure, we call ourselves a Christian nation; but far too often the phrase is a phrase only. Frequently in political life we give him standing room only. We open our congressional sessions with prayer and praise to Christ, but too often he is forgotten in subsequent legislation.

Public officials in high places take their oath of office with a hand resting upon the ancient Scriptures, but in too many instances fraud and corruption mark their administration.

In many areas of modern business there is standing room only for Christ. To be sure, there are wonderful business-men who are devoted Christians and who lift community life with their sense of integrity. Yet in far too many places there are those engaged in cutthroat methods and ruthless, unscrupulous competition.

And sometimes, sad to say, we give Christ standing room only in the church. When we think more of our machinery than of our message, we give him standing room only. When petty jealousy and bickering disrupt the fellowship, then we crowd out the Christ. When we let prejudice and pride take the place of bigness and humility, then there is no room for him.

But let us turn from this larger and general scene closer home, to ourselves, and see how in our personal lives we so often give him standing room only. Charles M. Crowe tells of an interesting operation performed in 1948 at Ohio State University. It seems that a stony sheath was removed from around the heart of a thirty-year-old man. When he was a boy, he was accidently shot while hunting, and the bullet pierced his heart. A protective lime covering formed over the heart and in time began to strangle it. The operation was a most delicate one and involved the separation of the ribs and the moving of the left lung to one side. Then the surgeon removed the stony sheath from the heart. The pressure was reduced, and almost immediately the heart began to expand and pump normally. "I feel a thousand per cent better already," the patient said when the operation was completed.

Our hearts over the years develop a hard protective coating because of hatred, bitterness, jealousy, envy, accumulated in the struggle of living. When we become preoccupied with our own little affairs, we forget God and "find it easier to sneer than to pray; simpler to work than to worship."

What we need, as Crowe reminds us, is a spiritual operation that only Christmas can perform when we dare surrender our heart's desires at the cradle of Bethlehem. Let us make room for him, for "without him life becomes stagnant and diseased, bitter and self-destructive." Let us give him more than standing room. Let us give him permanent occupation that life may be cleansed and purified, redeemed and restored, at Christmastime, for all time.

ON TAKING A CHANCE

"Push out to the deep water and lower your nets for a take."
Luke 5:4 (Moffatt)

IN THE fourth verse of the fifth chapter of Luke, Jesus says to Simon, "Push out to the deep water and lower your nets for a take." Here he is challenging his followers to take a chance in the deep waters where the fish are, to push out from shore and do business in big streams.

But Simon objected, saying, "Master, we worked all night and got nothing!" And then he said, "However, I will lower the nets at your command."

Let us look at this story and see how it applies to us today.

In the first place these disciples were willing to count God in while too many of us rule him out. They were willing to take a chance with God. Even against the experience of the past they followed his voice and launched out into the deep. We read, when they had followed his will, "they enclosed a huge shoal of fish."

It was an overwhelming experience for them. They took a chance on God and found that he made the difference. He made a difference in the use of their equipment. They had the same equipment, but it was under new direction. When it was put to the use which God demanded, then it served a great purpose. Where it had failed before, now it succeeded. Where it had come up empty, now it came up full.

This is a parable about modern life. Herein lies the answer to all the fear that is ours concerning atomic power and the mechanized age in which we live. To be sure, power misdirected leads to evil ends. Such power can be used as instruments for good or evil. It depends upon who is directing this power—whether God's way is heeded or whether the feeble wisdom of man, with all his weakness, is followed.

Harold C. Urey, winner of the Nobel prize in chemistry, has this to say:

There will never be a Maginot Line against the limitless powers of the Universe as developed by the limitless imagination of man. Our "defense" is in control—the safety of countries in the future, like our personal safety in cities, must rest on the law and the conscience of Man.

In the second place, although things weren't going right, these fishermen of Jesus kept on doing right.

These men must have reasoned with themselves: "Have we not toiled all night and caught nothing? Why should we fish any more today? Fish just won't bite. Why not go home and get to bed, rest from the night's labor? This is the sensible thing to do—quit now." But they didn't do this. They kept right on; they continued to fish.

There is no greater need in our time than that of doing right although everything seems to be going wrong. A verse of scripture reads: "If the foundations be destroyed, what can the righteous do?" There is only one answer to give. Just keep on being righteous.

One thing is certain: we cannot play with the eternal

laws of God. In the end they will prevail. The most dangerous attitude of our time is what is called "ethical subjectivism," expressed popularly in this way: There is nothing either good or bad, but thinking makes it so.

There are some truths which are eternally right. For example, cruelty to an innocent child is wrong not because custom says that it is, but because this is God's world and every child is made in his image and important in his sight.

When things seem to be going wrong, do not rule God out of the picture. Keep on doing right.

Two little girls were looking at a portrait of Queen Victoria in her royal robes. One asked the other, "What is she doing?"

The other replied, "She isn't doing anything. She is just reigning." But certainly we know that God does not just reign. He is active and reaches out to us all.

"Push out to the deep water and lower your nets for a take." This is our challenge. This is our call. We must be willing to take a chance on God, for when we do, we are not taking a chance but are merely resting our case in the hands of one who is in control, whose ways are beyond our ways, and whose purposes cannot be excelled.

VITAMINS FOR FAITH DEFICIENCIES

"They devoted themselves to the instruction given by the apostles and to fellowship, breaking bread and praying together."
Acts 2:42 (Moffatt)

IN THE fall of the year all of us concern ourselves with being built up for the winter. On most of our tables are little bottles containing iron, vitamins A, B-1, C, D, E. The children are given cod-liver oil. We adults take our pills to build bodies strong enough for winter living.

But today we want to talk about another type of deficiency —faith deficiencies. I guess all of us have felt at one time or another sort of run-down spiritually, when the zest for living had somehow ebbed away, when we lacked an awareness of God, when our faith was too weak to stand the day by day strain of living.

In Acts 2:41, 42, as translated by Moffatt, we find these words: "So those who accepted what he said were baptized; about three thousand souls were brought in, that day. They devoted themselves to the instruction given by the apostles and to fellowship, breaking bread and praying together."

From this verse we get four suggestions that can become for us vitamins for faith deficiencies.

In the first place these early Christians devoted themselves to instruction—they continued to learn; they built themselves up in the knowledge of the truth. What does this mean for us? Simply this—that if we are to hold the great securities of our faith intact, we must seek to know more about that faith. We must turn more often to the source book of our faith—the Bible.

No Christian who would keep his faith virile and vibrant and sufficient for the demands of day by day living can afford to neglect this chief vitamin of the soul, the Bible.

In the second place these early Christians devoted themselves to fellowship. They discovered that if they were to remain strong in the faith, they had to mingle with those who had the faith.

Certainly one of the ties that binds people to the church is fellowship, comradeship. You take fellowship out of a church, and what do you have left? It is void of life and warmth and feeling. You tie a newborn Christian into a friendly fellowship and wrap around his life joyous and wholesome associations, and his life will tend to grow strong and his religion meaningful.

A third way in which these early Christians were built up in the faith was in the breaking of bread. By this the writer is referring to frequent attendance at Communion.

This observance became for them a reminder of what Christ had done for them as well as a means of communicating with him. They found that the promise of his presence in this sacrament was fulfilled. Indeed, they met him there spiritually. Further, they dedicated themselves anew each time they broke bread in his name. From such solemn and sacred occasions they went away renewed.

We, too, today have that experience. Of course there are some who come and are not fed. This happened in

Jesus' day. Hundreds sat at his feet and listened to his matchless words and went away as cold as they were when they came. In this sacrament he offers us his presence and his strength, but those who come with closed minds and doubtful hearts go away hungry.

But those who "draw near with faith, and take this holy Sacrament to [their] comfort: and make [their] humble confession to Almighty God," go away strengthened and steadied for life's toil. We do not understand how it happens any more than we understand how today's food becomes part bone, part flesh, part blood, part waste—but we accept it through faith and in such acceptance find a vitamin for the spirit.

Finally these early Christians devoted themselves to praying together. They discovered that prayer is the very life line of the Christian's faith. They knew that if the vows taken at their baptism were to be kept intact, prayer was to be the cementing force. They knew that if they were to keep close to God, it would be through frequent communion with him.

All of us have had the experience of neglecting this important vitamin, and we have found ourselves getting away from the church, becoming critical of others, slipping into bad habits, losing touch with God.

Prayer strengthens life. Even our Lord himself found it to be important in his own life. Listen to his words: "I have meat to eat that ye know not of." Here Jesus is speaking of spiritual food, which brings nourishment even to tired muscles and fatigued bodies. Prayer became for him a plus, an over and above that saw him through. It was a reserve for tapping in hours of need.

Prayer can become that also for you and me—a vitamin for faith deficiencies.

ATTITUDES SHAPE LIFE

"God hath . . . given us the spirit . . . of power, and of love, and of a sound mind."   II Tim. 1:7

THE story of the faith and courage which sustained the crew in that momentous crash flight of Eddie Rickenbacker in the Pacific is an inspiring epic. After the rescue from drifting on a rubber raft for more than three weeks, Hans Christian Adamson, senior military observer, wrote his wife:

It would be difficult, or in fact impossible, for me to recall all our experiences. Just now I am trying to get a new outlook on life. . . .
On Friday afternoon we were spotted by a Marine Corps plane and later we were picked up, and you can't imagine the prayers of thanks we offered. While drifting was a horrible experience something wonderful has come of it. I have found a nearness to our Creator which I have never known before and I am certain that this new feeling is going to deeply affect both of our lives in the future.

In this unusual letter, following a trying experience, the words, "I am trying to get a new outlook on life," epitomize a real need in our time.

Indeed, the joy of living is determined not so much by what life brings to us but by the attitude we bring to life, not so much by what happens to us but by the way we look at what has happened.

Our living is determined more by our attitudes than by our ancestors. Great living comes with great outlooks.

What life does to us depends on what life finds in us, and what life finds in us is dependent on our outlooks, our attitudes, our motives.

One day my wife and I had lunch in the home of a lovely person. She has had trouble in her life. Illness has plagued her for over twelve years. But there is no trace of bitterness or complaint about her life. She is still grateful for the mercies of God and his marvelous goodness. I copied this verse from her kitchen wall before we left, for in it I detected an outlook which has given her victory:

> We'll therefore relish with content
> Whate'er kind Providence has sent.

This is not mere resignation to whatever life brings, not just passive acceptance; but it is seeing with creative eyes how even the evil and unwanted can be used for some good.

Victorious living has to do with outlook. Christianity is a way of looking at life through the eyes of Christ.

Paul in his letter to the Christians at Philippi said, "Let this mind be in you, which was also in Christ." He is saying, "Look at life through his eyes." What do we see?

We see that our problem is more mental than environmental, for Jesus brings new depth to life. He tells us that we are to be greater than anything that can happen to us, that we are to rise above our environment.

He is suggesting that we can often change our situation by changing our attitude toward it. Paul speaks of this when he reminds us that we are to be transformed by the renewing of our minds. In this depth to life which Jesus brings us we find resources which can help us remake the world and not allow the world to remake us.

John Homer Miller tells of a woman who lived unhappily in a New York apartment. She objected to the noise the people above her made. Finally after much effort she was able to get a different apartment in the same building. Before time to move she thought about the joy of getting away from the old place. In her joy she didn't notice the old annoyances. Her mind was already in her new home.

Then when the time came to move, she looked at her old apartment and saw its real advantages and concluded that it was better. She looked at it with a fresh mind, and it looked good to her. She stayed.

"Why," she exclaimed, "I didn't have to move into a new apartment. All I had to do was to move into a new mind."

What many of us need is a change of mind, not a change of environment.

A CLUB OR A CAUSE?

"Go ye therefore, and teach all nations."   Matt. 28:19

ONE day I was reading from the pen of a great Christian leader, and this arresting sentence caught my attention: "How do you think of the church and its world-wide service when you make out a check, as a club or as a cause?"

I have been thinking about this a great deal since then and conclude that as for me, today, the church is not a club but a cause.

Of course when we think of our friendly fellowship and the happy times we have together, we can see within the church some clublike features. Webster says that a club is "an association of persons for the promotion of some common object, as literature, good-fellowship, etc." But the church goes beyond the club idea, which has by its very nature limitations that must not be part of the church. Let us then consider some characteristics which make the church essentially a cause and not a club.

In the first place a club exists primarily for the benefit of its own members, whereas a church as a cause seeks as no other institution so little for itself and so much for others.

To be sure, there are benefits which can be compared to those offered in a club. But the church does not exist for itself but for what it can do through itself for others. The church as a cause seeks to be used as an instrument of God in the redemption of the world.

So the members of the church think in terms not merely

of what they get out of it but more of what can they put into it, not what are the returns that come their way but what can they send through it someone else's way.

In the second place a club usually has little interest beyond its own confines, whereas a church as a cause extends its interest to the uttermost parts of the world.

Our Lord, when he said, "Go ye therefore, and teach all nations, baptizing them in the name of the Father, and of the Son, and of the Holy Ghost," gave us our marching orders.

Thus the Christian church must have in the center of its life a warm, glowing concern that the gospel be spread both near and far. The church or the individual who is not interested in missions becomes a mission field. The man who cannot see beyond his own community and who does not recognize the claim that the gospel makes upon him to help spread it around the world—that man has failed to catch the spirit of Christ.

The quickest way to kill a church is to stop its outreach, to lose its concern in others beyond its borders, to fasten its eyes only on local matters. On the other hand the church which throbs with life and becomes a channel of power that sets men upon their feet again is the church whose heart reaches out to others, whose prayers include men in far-off places, whose giving goes beyond local needs.

Finally, a club solicits loyalty to a code, whereas a church introduces men to a person. It seeks to link the life of man with the life of God.

A club has as its head an earthly leader, but the church was instituted by God and is sustained by his living Spirit. A club is a man-made institution, while the church is divine in origin. It may be said in another way: a club has only a horizontal life while a church has both a horizontal as well as a vertical life, that is, a life related to God.

The church shares with other institutions in its horizontal life which moves from the past through the present into the future. But the real distinction of the church lies in what we might call the vertical life, its upward life.

It must actually be a bridge between heaven and earth. The church is not an end within itself but is rather an instrument to help men contact God. It is here we should assemble with the purpose of worshiping God, of feeling his presence. It is a place where we should be inspired to do noble things, to see what should be done, and not only that but receive that power which is needed to do those noble things.

Thus the Christian church is not a club but a cause, seeking to link the life of man with the Spirit of God.

LIFE—A CONTINUOUS STORY

"Because I live, ye shall live also."　　　　John 14:19

ALL of us are confronted at one time or another with questions like these: Is life a continuous story? Is there a reality beyond the grave? To be sure, hope and faith in life after death cannot be verified as a cold scientific fact, yet there are evidences pointing definitely in that direction.

In the first place the reality of the unseen world points toward a future life. No longer can men deny the existence of two worlds—the material and the spiritual. No longer can skeptics say that there is nothing to life but material substance. Arthur Stanley Eddington, one of the world's greatest scientists, says in his book, *Science and the Unseen World*: "We are no longer tempted to condemn the spiritual aspects of our nature as illusory because of their lack of concreteness. We have traveled far from the standpoint which identifies the real with the concrete." To be a realist today a man must admit that the most basic aspects of life cannot be seen with the eye, but are spiritual.

In the second place the incompleteness of life makes us believe in immortality. These spirits of ours only taste the riches of this life. Many there are who are snuffed out long before their candle has consumed the wax. Even those who linger to riper years find that "one lifetime is not enough," for life is only beginning as it apparently is ending. Yes, life is too incomplete for me to believe this is all.

A third evidence making me feel that life is a continuous story is the people we have known who were so genuinely good. It is impossible to think of their "spirits being blown out like a candle in the wind." Professor Palmer of Harvard gave this assurance in speaking of his lovely wife, Alice Freeman Palmer, when she died. He wrote: "I refuse to believe that I live in a universe which, out of deference to a few misplaced particles of matter, would exclude so fair a spirit." Surely he could not have proved that by logic, arithmetic, or chemistry; but he had a deep indwelling feeling that a person like that could not die.

You too know people whose spirits and natures are so fine that it doesn't make sense for this brief stay here to be all. No, we are sure the best will not be lost.

Finally the most important evidence must be added—our faith in the goodness of God. Our whole conception of the future life is intertwined with this faith. All thought and discussion end in the nature and character of God.

For life's best portrait of what God is like we turn our thoughts and hopes to Jesus the Christ. Surely if, as he said, the very hairs of our heads are numbered and the paths of our feet guided, if around these mortal lives is everlasting mercy, then certainly a God who cares like that is one who has plans for the silence, the dim unknown. Yes, if God cared so much for his children as to send a Son and permit him to suffer a cruel death on a cross so that men might see the light, then surely a heart which cares like that is one which gave Jesus authority to say, "In my Father's house are many mansions. . . . I go to prepare a place for you. . . . Because I live, ye shall live also."

INDEX